A Concise Guide to Catholic Social Teaching

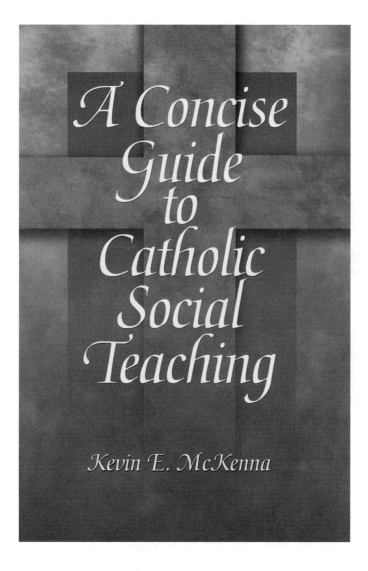

A Concise Guide to Catholic Social Teaching

Kevin E. McKenna

ave maria press   Notre Dame, Indiana

© 2002 by Ave Maria Press, Inc.

All rights reserved. No part of this book may be used or reproduced in any manner whatsoever, except in the case of reprints in the context of reviews, without written permission from Ave Maria Press, Inc., P.O. Box 428, Notre Dame, IN 46556.

www.avemariapress.com

International Standard Book Number: 0-87793-979-9

Cover and text design by Katherine Robinson Coleman

Printed and bound in the United States of America.

Library of Congress Cataloging-in-Publication Data

McKenna, Kevin E., 1950-

A concise guide to Catholic social teaching / Kevin E. McKenna.

p. cm.

Includes bibliographical references and index.

ISBN 0-87793-979-9 (pbk.)

1. Sociology, Christian (Catholic) 2. Catholic

Church--Doctrines. I.
Title.

BX1753 .M38 2002

261.8'088'22--dc21

200200677

CIP

Dedicated in memory of

D ENNIS W. H ICKEY

Auxiliary Bishop of Rochester

A true gentleman and a scholar

Requiescat in pace

CONTENTS

4: Option for the Poor and Vulnerable 57

7: Care for God's Creation   117

Appendix   125

One of the most important contributions made by the Roman Catholic Church during the last one hundred and ten years has been the development of a strong Catholic social teaching. Based on the scriptures, Christian and Hebrew, several recent popes have articulated a passionate response to various social issues that developed during the industrialized world of the late nineteenth and twentieth centuries. The teachings have taken a variety of forms, primarily encyclicals—a formal papal presentation related to some particular teaching, intended to present the church's position regarding some issue of concern. Beginning with Leo XIII and his encyclical *Rerum Novarum* (1891), which addressed some of the problems that were emerging in the relationship of management and labor due to the great changes brought about by the Industrial Age, every pope thereafter would utilize his office to address pressing social concerns.

A Concise Guide to Catholic Social Teaching is an effort to distill the teachings of major papal teachings as well as teachings from the episcopal conference of the United States into summary form. It is not an exhaustive summary of Catholic social teaching but rather presents several major church documents that have provided clear guidance in regard to perplexing social issues. Included are several pastoral letters and responses from the U.S. hierarchy often built upon the encyclical teachings, making them relevant to the local scene by providing concrete domestic applications. These documents have been summarized and paraphrased, while hopefully maintaining the strength and vigor of the original, which should always be consulted as the official teaching. It is hoped, however, that the reader nonetheless will obtain a useful sense of these milestone developments in Catholic social thought. The numbers of the sections summarized from the original document are provided throughout. Occasionally exact section references are omitted when not supplied in the original document. Such summaries will highlight several themes, including the dignity of the worker and laborer, human dignity and respect for life, and economic justice. The

United States bishops, in their document *Sharing Catholic Social Teaching: Challenges and Directions* (1998), provided a key framework for discussing Catholic social teaching:

Life and the Dignity of the Human Person

Call to Family, Community, and Participation

Rights and Responsibilities

Option for the Poor and Vulnerable

The Dignity of Work and the Right of Workers

Solidarity

Care for God's Creation

These themes have served as the locus for summarizing the documents presented in this work. At times, similar themes are repeated in several documents. I have chosen, for the most part, to divide the documents, usually in their entirety, under the broad theme it seems most naturally to be identified with.

The church since the Second Vatican Council has become particularly concerned with the need to promote Catholic social teaching. Toward that end, many parishes have developed "social action committees" or their equivalents. These groups have been very effective, for example, in mobilizing parish resources to provide economic assistance to those who are in financial need in their parish, local area, or diocese; as well as those who are in urgent need in some area in the United States, or even somewhere else in the world, e.g., after a major catastrophic disaster. However commendable or laudatory these initiatives, it can sometimes happen that efforts are focused on the *results* while losing sight of the rationale for the works of gospel justice. A careful, consistent, and frequent reflection on the themes of justice and charity that are such predominant themes of the scriptures and, consequently, the social teachings of the church can be a helpful resource, combining prayer and action. In addition, such reflection and study can encourage new initiatives, as parish committees (or even parish pastoral councils) review the concrete proposals and suggestions that are often recommended in the various church documents.

A Concise Guide to Catholic Social Teaching

The uses of this book are not limited to parishes. It can also be used with effectiveness by diocesan social ministry offices, e.g., Catholic Charities, who do on a larger scale what is often done by individual parishes. Religious orders, which often have committees or similar structures organized for coordinating the social concerns of their particular community, should find such a reference tool helpful for their work, especially in their efforts to "raise consciousness" within their communities (and subsequently, to the wider world) to the concerns of social justice.

Concluding each chapter is a series of questions, designed and presented with the hope that they might stimulate some appropriate reflection on the theme presented in the document. A parish council, for example, might find it useful to begin its regularly scheduled meeting with some type of "continuing education." This could be accomplished by assigning one of the chapters of this book for reading before the next meeting, and then using the study questions (or a question) to be shared for a few minutes as time allows. In this way, the council is exposed gradually to some of the major themes of Catholic social teaching and is pressed to consider how these teachings can be put concretely into practice within a parish setting. Such a procedure can easily be expanded and adapted to be utilized by any parish committee or organization, e.g., evangelization, Christian formation, etc. Just as it is important that we *act* on behalf of the gospel of Jesus, so too is it important that we know *why* we are doing what we do.

This work is also intended for use by the busy pastoral minister, providing a preaching resource that can be helpful in addressing the social concerns that are raised in the scriptures. Various homiletic themes related to Catholic social teachings are identified by reference to the Sunday lectionary of Mass readings. Thus, during the course of scriptural exposition and teaching that occupies the homilist during the course of the liturgical year, suggested linkages with the heritage of social teachings are provided (see appendix, pp. 132-139).

In the appendix can also be found a "Reconciliation Service for Justice and Peace," which can be adapted for use in a variety of settings. Many parish communities gather during the Advent and Lenten seasons to celebrate God's plentiful mercy.

A parish may wish to utilize a continuing education program or a retreat experience during these sacred times to study Catholic social teaching. The service provided here can conclude such programs by providing an opportunity for personal and communal reflection, leading to a service of reconciliation in the area of social justice.

Also in the appendix biographical information will be found on the various popes who have most recently contributed with their encyclicals to our Catholic social tradition. The creation of the teaching of the church did not come from a vacuum. In a certain sense, the popes have translated a *sensus fidelium* (sense of the faithful) about important areas of justice and love of neighbor into a strong critique that provides a clear and consistent teaching framed within the gospel imperatives. It can be helpful, in studying the development of Catholic social teaching, to know something of the background of those who have influenced the production of important teachings, as well as the times in which they lived.

Finally, a glossary of terms is provided which highlights certain terms used in the text that may not be immediately understandable, due to their almost exclusive use with a social gospel teaching context. A short description of the documents referenced in this work can be found as well in the glossary.

I am grateful to those who have assisted me in this project, especially as they have attempted to live the message of these profound church teachings in their daily lives. I am particularly indebted to Dr. Marvin Krier Mich and Dr. Patricia Schoelles, who were kind enough to review the manuscript and offer invaluable guidance, direction, and suggestions.

May the Lord bless the efforts of all those who work to be a light to the nations of God's saving love, mercy, and justice. May the insights and teachings of the church in regard to its social mission given by Christ continue to move us all to be witnesses of the Master to a world that seeks so consistently to find him.

BSTU Brothers and Sisters to Us

CA   On the Hundredth Anniversary of *Rerum Novarum*, *Centesimus Annus*

CP   The Challenge of Peace: God's Promise and Our Response, a Pastoral Letter on War and Peace

CPUN Statement on Capital Punishment

EJFA Economic Justice for All

EV   The Gospel of Life, *Evangelium Vitae*

LE   On Human Work, *Laborem Exercens*

MM   On Christianity and Social Progress, *Mater et Magistra*

PP   The Development of Peoples, *Populorum Progressio*

PT   Peace on Earth, *Pacem in Terris*

QA   On Reconstructing the Social Order, *Quadragesimo Anno*

RN   The Condition of Labor, *Rerum Novarum*

SRS   On Social Concern, *Sollicitudo Rei Socialis*

CHAPTER 1

Life and the Dignity of the Human Person

The church has proclaimed as a basic principle of its social teaching that each person is created in the image of God. It is the responsibility of every society to ensure that human life is protected from the moment of conception until natural death. The summaries that follow are taken from Brothers and Sisters to Us: U.S. Bishops' Pastoral Letter on Racism, *1979;* The U.S. Bishops' Statement on Capital Punishment *issued in November 1980; and the encyclical of Pope John Paul II,* Evangelium Vitae, *March 25, 1995.*

BROTHERS AND SISTERS TO US
U.S. BISHOPS

Racism is an evil that endures in our society, despite advances and significant changes in the last two decades. The majority of Americans realize that discrimination is both unjust and unworthy of this nation.

It cannot be denied that the ugly external features of racism that marred our society in the past have in part been eliminated. At the same time, however, it cannot be denied that too often what has happened has been only a covering over and not a fundamental change. The climate of crisis engendered by demonstrations and protests has given way to a mood of indifference. (BSTU)

Racial and Economic Justice

Attention should be called to the persistent presence of racism and in particular to the relationship between racial and economic justice. Although racism and economic oppression are distinct, they are interrelated forces that can dehumanize our society.

Major segments of the population are being pushed to the margins of society. As economic pressures tighten, racial minorities slip further into the unending cycle of poverty, deprivation, ignorance, disease, and crime. (BSTU)

The Church and Prejudice

The church cannot remain silent about racial injustices in society and in its own structures. Discrimination belies our civil tradition and constitutional heritage that recognizes the equality, dignity, and inalienable rights of all its citizens. We are, as well, heirs of a religious teaching that proclaims that all men and women, as children of God, are brothers and sisters.

Racism is a sin that divides the human family by proclaiming that some human beings are inherently superior because of race. It is a denial of the truth of the dignity of each human being revealed by the mystery of the Incarnation.

We look to Christ for the strength to overcome racism. In Christ Jesus "there is neither Jew nor Greek, male nor female; for all are one . . . " (Gal 3:28). In Christ Jesus the church finds the central cause for its commitment to justice and the struggle for the human rights and dignity of all persons. (BSTU)

Presence of Racism in the United States Today

The continuing existence of racism in our country is apparent when we look beneath the surface of our national life as, for example, in the case of unemployment figures. For decades, denied access to opportunities has been for minority families a crushing burden. Racism can also be seen in housing patterns in our major cities and suburbs. The gap between rich and poor is widening, not decreasing.

Racism can be noted in the disproportionate minority population in prison and the violent crime that is the daily companion of a life of poverty and deprivation. The victims of such crimes are disproportionately non-white and poor. Racism is also apparent in the attitudes of and behavior of some law enforcement officials and the unequal availability of legal assistance.

Racism is sometimes apparent in the growing sentiment that too much is being given to racial minorities by way of affirmative action programs or allocations to address long-standing imbalances in minority representation and government-funded programs for the disadvantaged. At times, protestations that claim that all persons should be treated equally reflect the desire to maintain a status quo favoring one race and social group at the expense of the poor and the non-white.

The contribution of each racial minority is distinctive and rich. Each racial group has sunk its roots deep in the soil of our culture and has contributed in some way to giving this country its unique character and diverse coloration.

Racism is manifest in the tendency to stereotype and marginalize whole segments of the population whose presence is seen as a threat. It can be seen in the indifference given to the minority poor often perceived by some as expendable. The new face of racism is the computer printout, the graph of profits and losses, the pink slip, the nameless statistic. Racism today flourishes in the triumph of private concern over public responsibility, individual success over social commitment, and personal fulfillment over authentic compassion. (BSTU)

Christian Response to Racism

New forms of racism must be brought face to face with the figure of Christ. The Christian response to the challenges of our times is to be found in the good news of Jesus. God's word proclaims the oneness of the human family. All are created in the image of God. The church is truly universal, embracing all races. The church has a duty to proclaim the truth about the human being as disclosed in the truth about Jesus Christ.

Catholics must acknowledge a share in the mistakes and sins of the past, as prisoners of fear and prejudice. At times conformity to social pressures has replaced compliance with social justice.

The prophetic voice of the church must not be muted—especially not by the counterwitness of some of its own people. The church must strive to make every element of human life correspond to the true dignity of the human person. The church must continue to proclaim that the sin of racism defiles the image of God and degrades the sacred dignity of humankind, revealed in the mystery of the Incarnation.

Conversion is the continuing task of each Christian. Christians must try to influence the attitudes of others by expressly rejecting racial stereotypes, racist jokes, slurs, and remarks. It is important to become more sensitive as to how social structures inhibit the economic, educational, and social advancement of the poor, and to commit to work with others in political efforts to bring about changes on behalf of justice.

Particular care should be taken to foster vocations among minority groups. There should also be a fostering of spiritual gifts of the various races and peoples within the liturgy as noted in the *Constitution on the Sacred Liturgy* (10, 37, 39, 40).

Special attention should be given to the plight of undocumented workers. Catholic institutions that are employers should examine carefully their policies to see that they faithfully conform to the church's teaching on justice for workers and respect their rights. Investment portfolios should be examined to determine whether racist institutions and policies are inadvertently being supported.

It is recommended that Catholic institutions avoid the services of agencies and industries which refuse to take affirmative action to achieve equal opportunity and that the church itself always be a model as an equal opportunity employer.

Leadership training programs should be established on the local level in order to encourage effective leadership among racial minorities on all levels of the church, local as well as national.

Active spiritual and financial support should be given to associations and institutions organized by Catholic blacks, Hispanics,

Native Americans, and Asians within the church for the promotion of ministry to and by their respective communities.

There should be a continuation and expansion of Catholic schools in the inner cities and other disadvantaged areas. The church in the United States has been distinguished by its efforts to educate the poor and disadvantaged.

The difficulties of these new times demand a new vision and renewed courage to transform our society. Globally, we live in an interdependent community of nations; those nations, which possess more of the world's riches, must share with those in serious need. The private sector should be aware of its responsibility to promote racial justice and promote genuine development in poor societies.

There must be no turning back along the road to justice. (BSTU).

STATEMENT ON CAPITAL PUNISHMENT
U.S. BISHOPS

Criticisms of the criminal justice system in the United States call for careful and prayerful reflection on the question of capital punishment by the Christian community, showing a respect and concern for the rights of all. The public debate about capital punishment deals with values of the utmost importance: respect for the sanctity of human life, the protection of human life, the preservation of order in society, and the achievement of justice through law. Many factors must be considered, including the need to provide safety for members of society and concern for the law enforcement officers who may be endangered in the midst of violent crime. There are no simple answers to this complex topic, but it is necessary to look to the claims of justice and to the example and teaching of Jesus. (CPUN)

Purposes of Punishment

Catholic teaching has accepted the principle that the state has the right to take the life of a person guilty of an extremely serious crime and that the state may take appropriate measures to protect itself and its citizens from grave harm. The question for judgment is whether capital punishment is justifiable under present circumstances.

Since punishment involves the deliberate infliction of evil on another, it is always in need of justification. The three traditional justifications advanced for punishment are retribution, deterrence, and reform.

The deterrence of actual or potential criminals from future deeds of violence by the threat of capital punishment is far from certain. There are strong reasons to doubt that many crimes of violence are undertaken in a spirit of rational calculation. Reform cannot be used as justification for capital punishment since it necessarily deprives the criminal of the opportunity to develop a new way of life. Although the need for retribution or the restoration of order justifies punishment, it does not need or require taking the life of a criminal.

The forms and limits of punishment must be determined by moral objectives which go beyond the mere infliction of injury on the guilty.

The forms of punishment must be determined with a view to the protection of society, the reformation of the criminal, and his or her reintegration into society (which may not be possible in certain situations).

In the conditions of contemporary American society, the legitimate purposes of punishment do not justify the imposition of the death penalty. There are serious considerations which should prompt Christians and all Americans to support the abolition of capital punishment. (CPUN)

Christian Values in the Abolition of Capital Punishment

The abolition of the death penalty would promote values that are important to Christian citizens. Abolition sends a message that the cycle of violence can be broken, that it is not necessary to take life for life, and that more humane and effective responses can be envisioned in response to violent crime.

It is also a manifestation of the belief in the unique worth and dignity of each person from the moment of conception, a creature made in the image and likeness of God.

It is also further testimony that God is the Lord of life. It is also consonant with the example of Jesus who both taught and practiced the forgiveness of injustice and who came to "give his life as a ransom for many" (Mk 10:45). (CPUN)

Difficulties Inherent in Capital Punishment

Infliction of the death penalty extinguishes the possibilities of reform and rehabilitation for the person executed as well as the opportunity to make some creative compensation for the evil that has been done.

It also involves the possibility of mistake, which cannot be totally eliminated from the justice system.

It also involves long and unavoidable delays, a consequence of necessary safeguards, but it can also produce aimlessness, fear, and despair in the criminal on death row.

The actual carrying out of the death penalty can bring with it great and avoidable anguish for the criminal, his or her family and loved ones, and those who are called on to perform or to witness the execution.

Executions attract enormous publicity, much of it unhealthy, stirring up considerable acrimony in public discussion.

There is also widespread belief that many convicted criminals are sentenced to death in an unfair and discriminatory manner. The legal system and the criminal justice system both work in a society which bears in its psychological, social, and economic patterns the mark of racism. Those condemned to die are nearly always poor and are disproportionately black. (CPUN)

Conclusions

The abolition of the death penalty is not proposed as a simple solution to the problems of crime and punishment. There is a special need to offer sympathy to and support for the victims of violent crime and their families. A firm resolution is needed that help will be given to the victims of violent crimes and their families. It is the special responsibility of the church to provide a community of faith and trust in which God's grace can heal the personal and spiritual wounds of those victimized.

Important changes are needed in the correctional system in order to make it truly conducive to the reform and rehabilitation of convicted criminals and their reintegration into society. Also to be emphasized is the importance of restricting the easy availability of guns and other weapons of violence. Opposition must be made against the glamorizing of violence in entertainment with its detrimental effect on children. Educational efforts must be undertaken to promote respect for the human dignity of all people.

We are called to contemplate the crucified Christ who set us the supreme example of forgiveness and of the triumph of compassionate love. (CPUN)

THE GOSPEL OF LIFE, *EVANGELIUM VITAE*
POPE JOHN PAUL II

The gospel of life is at the heart of Jesus' message. In presenting the heart of his redemptive mission, Jesus says: "I came that they may have life, and have it abundantly" (Jn 10:10). Believers in Christ must defend and promote the right to life. Through his incarnation, the Son of God has united himself in some fashion with every human being and established the incomparable value of every human person. The gospel of God's love for each person, the gospel of the dignity of the person, and the gospel of life are a single and indivisible gospel. (EV 1-3)

The proclamation of life is ever more urgent due to the increase and gravity of threats to the life of individuals and peoples. For example, broad sectors of public opinion justify certain crimes against life in the name of the rights of individual freedom. Such initiatives are even being given cognizance by legislators in many countries. The individual conscience is finding it more and more difficult to distinguish between good and evil in what concerns the basic value of human life. (EV 4)

A Concise Guide to Catholic Social Teaching

Present-Day Threats to Human Life

The gospel of life proclaimed in the beginning when human beings were created in the image of God is contradicted by the painful experience of death which enters the world. Death entered the world in a violent way through the killing of Abel by his brother Cain. Like the first fratricide, every murder is a violation of the spiritual kinship uniting humankind in one family. All kinds of ideologies can attempt to justify and disguise atrocious crimes against human beings.

God is merciful, even when he punishes. He places a mark on Cain lest anyone who comes upon him should kill him (Gn 4:15). In this, the paradoxical mystery of the merciful justice of God is shown.

Attacks against human life still continue through human history, from a variety of sources, including murder, war, slaughter, and genocide. Violence continues against children who are forced into poverty, malnutrition, and hunger due to an unjust distribution of resources.

Attacks by the State

There is another category of attacks which affects life in its earliest and in its final stages. In many cases the state gives these attacks legal recognition and makes them available through the free services of health-care personnel. Such attacks strike human life at its greatest frailty, when it lacks any means of self-defense.

There are many factors involved, including a profound crisis of culture, the complexity of society, acute poverty, and anxiety or frustration in which the struggle to make ends meet can make the choice to defend life so demanding as sometimes to reach the point of heroism.

Culture of Death

There has been an emergence of a veritable structure of sin in the form of a "culture of death," a war of the powerful against the weak. A life which would require greater acceptance, love, and care is considered useless, or held to be an intolerable burden, and is therefore rejected in one way or another.

To facilitate abortion, enormous sums of money have been invested in pharmaceutical products, which can kill the fetus without recourse to any medical assistance. Such developments become capable of removing abortion from any kind of control or social responsibility.

The Pro-Abortion Culture

The pro-abortion culture is especially strong where the church's teaching on contraception is rejected. In some instances, contraception and abortion are rooted in a hedonistic mentality unwilling to accept responsibility in matters of sexuality. The life which could result from a sexual encounter becomes an enemy to be avoided at all costs, and abortion becomes the only possible decisive response to failed contraception. Prenatal diagnosis all too often becomes an opportunity for proposing and procuring an abortion.

Serious threats hang over the incurably ill and the dying as well. Culture today considers any suffering as the epitome of evil, to be eliminated at all costs. Euthanasia is sometimes justified by a utilitarian motive of avoiding costs which bring no return and which weigh heavily on society.

There is also a "demographic" argument made today in support of attacks against life. The more powerful countries fear that the most prolific and poorest people represent a threat to the well-being and peace of their own countries. Sometimes, the economic help that the richer countries could provide is made conditional on the acceptance of an anti-birth policy.

The Right to Life

The process that once led to discovering the idea of "human rights"—rights inherent in every person—is today marked by a surprising contradiction. In an age when the inviolable rights of the person are solemnly proclaimed and the value of life is publicly affirmed, the very right to life is being denied or trampled upon, especially at the moment of birth and the moment of death. The roots of this remarkable contradiction lie in today's cultural and moral nature. There exists a mentality of extreme subjectivism which recognizes as a subject of rights only the person who enjoys full or at least incipient autonomy and who emerges from a state of total dependence on others. There is also a mentality today which tends to equate personal dignity with the capacity for verbal and explicit communication. There is, therefore, in this thinking no room for the one who is a weak element in the social structure.

This is the exact opposite of what a state ruled by law is historically intended to affirm. When freedom, out of a desire to emancipate itself from all forms of tradition and authority, shuts out the most obvious evidence of an objective and universal truth, then the person ends up no longer taking as the point of reference for choices the truth about good and evil. Rather, the criterion becomes only a subjective and changeable opinion—selfish interest and whim.

Such a view of freedom leads to a distortion of life in society, a mass of individuals placed side by side but without any mutual bonds. Social life ventures on to the shifting sands of relativism. Everything is negotiable, everything is open to bargaining—even the first of the fundamental rights, the right to life.

Simultaneously, there is within culture an eclipse of the sense of God and of the human. When a sense of God is lost in a secularized culture, the sense of the human being is also threatened—the human no longer sees the transcendent character of the human being. In such a context, suffering, a factor of possible personal growth, is always seen as an evil, to be opposed and avoided. The body is seen then as pure materiality, a complex of organs, functions, and energies to be used, according to the sole criteria of pleasure and efficiency. Sexuality is depersonalized and exploited. Interpersonal relations are seriously impoverished.

Christ's blood reveals to humanity the greatness of the human being and the true vocation: the sincere gift of self. The blood of Christ is the instrument of communion, the richness of life for all. It is from the blood of Christ that all people draw the strength to commit themselves to promoting life. The unconditional choice for life reaches its full religious and moral meaning when it flows from, is formed by, and is nourished by faith in Christ. The church is becoming more aware of the grace and responsibility that come to it from the Lord of proclaiming, celebrating, and serving the gospel of life. (EV 7-9, 11, 13, 15, 16, 18-23, 25, 28)

The Christian Message Concerning Life

The gospel of life is concrete and personal, consisting of the proclamation of the person of Jesus, who said, "I am the way and the truth and the life" (Jn 14:6). Through the words, actions, and person of Jesus, humanity is given the possibility of knowing the complete truth concerning the value of human life. It can also be known in its essential traits by human reason.

The fullness of the gospel message about life was prepared for in the Old Testament. The Lord revealed himself to Israel as its Savior, with the power to ensure a future to those without hope. In coming to know the value of its own existence as a people, Israel grows in its perception of the meaning and value of life itself.

Revelation progressively allows the first notion of immortal life planted by the Creator in the human heart to be grasped with ever-greater clarity.

Jesus and the Proclamation of Human Dignity

Just as God reassured Israel in the midst of danger, so the Son of God proclaims to all who feel threatened and hindered that their lives are a good to which the Father's love gives meaning and value. The crowds of the sick and the outcasts who follow him and seek him out find in Jesus' words and actions a revelation of the great value of their lives and of how their hope of salvation is well founded. It is by his death that Jesus reveals the entire splendor and value of life.

The human being has been given a sublime dignity based on the intimate bond that unites each individual to God: in the human being shines forth a reflection of God. All who commit themselves to following Christ are given the fullness of life: the divine image is restored, renewed, and brought to perfection in them. Whoever believes in Jesus and enters into communion with him has eternal life because that person hears from Jesus the only words that reveal and communicate to his existence the fullness of life. The dignity of this life is linked not only to its beginning, to the fact that it comes from God, but also to its final end, to its destiny of fellowship with God in knowledge and love of him.

God is the sole Lord of this life. But God does not exercise this power in an arbitrary and threatening manner, but rather as part of his care and loving concern for his creatures. The sacredness of life gives way to its inviolability. The commandment "You shall not kill," included and more fully expressed in the positive command of love for one's neighbor, is reaffirmed in all its force by the Lord Jesus. The deepest element of God's commandment to protect human life is the requirement to show reverence and love for every person. To defend and promote life, to show reverence and love for it, is a task that God entrusts to every person.

The mission of Jesus, with the many healings he performed, shows God's great concern even for the individual's bodily life. No one can arbitrarily choose whether to live or die. The absolute master of such a decision is the Creator alone.

By his death, Jesus sheds light on the meaning of the life and death of every human being. Life finds its center, its meaning, and its fulfillment when it is given up. (EV 29, 31, 32, 36-39, 41, 47, 50)

God's Holy Law

The gospel of life is both a great gift of God and an exacting task for humanity. Scripture presents the precept "You shall not kill" as a divine commandment. God proclaims that he is the absolute Lord of the life of each individual, and thus human life is given a sacred and inviolable character. The commandment not to kill implicitly encourages a positive attitude of absolute respect for life.

The Death Penalty

Legitimate defense is not only a right but also a duty for someone responsible for another's life. Unfortunately it sometimes happens that the need to render the aggressor incapable of causing harm sometimes involves taking a life.

The problem of the death penalty should be examined in the context of a system of penal justice ever more in line with human dignity and with God's plan for humanity and society. Public authority must redress the violation of personal and social rights by imposing on the offender an adequate punishment for the crime, as a condition for the offender to regain the exercise of his or her freedom. The public authority therefore defends the public order and ensures people's safety while offering the offender an incentive to change his or her behavior. For these purposes to be achieved the nature and extent of the punishment must be carefully evaluated and decided upon. The punishment ought not to go to the extreme of executing the offender except in cases of absolute necessity: when it would not be possible otherwise to defend society. Today such cases are very rare, if not practically nonexistent.

Faced with the progressive weakening of individual consciences and in society of the sense of the absolute and grave moral illicitness of the direct taking of all innocent human life, the church's magisterium has spoken out with increasing frequency in defense of the sacredness and inviolability of human life. *The direct and voluntary killing of an innocent human being is always gravely immoral.* No one can in any way permit the killing of an innocent human being whether a fetus or an embryo, an infant or an adult, an old person or one suffering from an incurable disease, or a person who is dying. Furthermore, no one is permitted to ask for this act of killing, either for himself or herself or for another person entrusted to his or her care, nor can he or she consent to it, either explicitly or implicitly. Nor can any authority legitimately recommend or permit such an action.

The Crime of Abortion

Among all the crimes which can be committed against human life, procured abortion is particularly serious and deplorable. Today, in many people's minds, the perception of its gravity has become progressively obscured. The moral gravity is apparent if we realize that we are dealing with murder since the one being eliminated is a human being at the very beginning of life. No one more absolutely innocent could be imagined.

Sometimes the decision made by the mother for an abortion is not made for purely selfish motives; however, that can never justify the deliberate killing of an innocent human being.

Others can influence a decision to have an abortion, including the father, the wider family circle, and friends. Also responsible can be legislators who promote and approve abortion laws, and health-care facilities and their personnel where abortions are performed. Even culture and society have an effect when it encourages sexual permissiveness.

Some attempt to justify abortion by claiming that the result of conception, at least up to a certain number of days, cannot be considered a personal human life. But from the time that the ovum is fertilized, a life is begun which is neither that of the mother or father. It is the life of a new human being with its own growth. The human being must be respected and treated as a person from the moment of conception.

Embryo Experimentation

The evaluation of the morality of abortion is to be applied also to intervention on human embryos. The use of human embryos or fetuses as an object of experimentation constitutes a crime against their dignity as human beings who have a right to the same respect owed to a child once born, just as to every person. Also to be condemned are procedures that exploit living human embryos and fetuses "produced" for this purpose by *in vitro* fertilization—either to be used as "biological material" or as providers of organs or tissue for transplants in the treatment of certain diseases. The killing of innocent human creatures, even if carried out to help others, constitutes an absolutely unacceptable act.

Prenatal Diagnostic Techniques

Attention must be given to evaluating the morality of prenatal diagnostic techniques. Sometimes it happens that these techniques are used with the intention to accept selective abortion in order to prevent the birth of children affected by various types of anomalies. This attitude is seen as reprehensible, since it presumes to measure the value of human life only within the parameters of "normality" and physical well-being.

Euthanasia

To many today, life seems valued only to the extent that it brings pleasure and well-being. Suffering seems like an unbearable setback. Death is considered "senseless" if it suddenly interrupts a life still open to a future of new and interesting experiences. But it becomes a "rightful liberation" when life is seen as no longer meaningful because it is filled with pain and doomed to even greater suffering.

There can be a temptation to have recourse to euthanasia, to take control of death and bring it about before its time. Euthanasia must be distinguished from the decision to forego so-called "aggressive medical treatment," when it is seen as disproportionate to any expected results or because it imposes an excessive burden on the patient and his or her family. In such situations, when death is clearly imminent and inevitable, one can in conscience refuse forms of treatment that would only secure a precarious and burdensome prolongation of life so long as the normal care due to the sick person is not interrupted. It is licit to relieve pain by various types of painkillers and sedatives, even when this risks the shortening of life. In such a case, death is not sought, but rather simply a desire to ease pain effectively.

Suicide

Suicide is always a morally objectionable choice, since it represents a rejection of God's absolute sovereignty over life and death. To concur with the intention of another to commit suicide and to help in carrying it out through so-called "assisted suicide" means to cooperate and at times be the actual perpetrator of an injustice. True compassion leads to sharing another's pain. It does not kill the person whose suffering we cannot bear. The height of arbitrariness and injustice is reached when certain people, such as physicians or legislators, arrogate to themselves the power to decide who ought to live and who ought to die.

Proclaiming the Right to Life in a Democratic Society

In the democratic culture of our time it is commonly held that the legal system of any society should limit itself to taking account of and accepting the convictions of the majority. At the basis of these tendencies is an ethical relativism that characterizes much of present-day culture. Democracy cannot be idolized to the point of making it a substitute for morality or a panacea for immorality. The moral values of a democracy are not automatic; rather, democracy depends on conformity to the moral law, the "natural law" written in the human heart, to which it must be subject. There is therefore a need to recover the basic elements of a vision of the relationship between civil law and moral law. Civil law must ensure that all members of society enjoy respect for certain fundamental rights, which innately belong to the person, rights that every positive law must guarante. First and fundamental among these is the inviolable right to life of every innocent human life.

Abortion and euthanasia are crimes that no human law can claim to legitimize. There is no obligation in conscience to obey such laws; instead there is a grave and clear obligation to oppose them by conscientious objection.

Christians are called upon under grave obligation of conscience not to cooperate formally in practices that, even if permitted by civil legislation, are contrary to God's law. To refuse to take part in committing an injustice is not only a moral duty but also a basic human right.

The commandment "You shall not kill" even in its more positive aspects of respecting, loving, and promoting human life is binding on every individual human being. (EV 52, 54, 56-60, 63-66, 69-71, 73, 74, 77)

Toward a New Culture of Human Life

The gospel of Christ has been received by the church as a gift. The church exists in order to evangelize, to proclaim the gospel message. The gospel of life is an integral part of the Gospel that is Jesus Christ himself. Everyone has a responsibility of being at the service of this gospel of life, which proclaims that human life, as a gift from God, is sacred and inviolable. In preaching such a gospel, we must not fear hostility or unpopularity, and we must refuse any compromise or ambiguity, which might conform us to the world's way of thinking.

Education in Values

Education aimed at encouraging vocations to service and practical projects inspired by the gospel are needed. Agencies and centers of service to life need to be directed by people who are fully aware of the importance of the gospel of life. To implement the gospel of life requires certain forms of social activity and commitment in the political field. Civil leaders particularly have a duty to make courageous choices in support of life. Likewise, on the issue of population growth, public authorities have a responsibility always to take into account and respect the primary and inalienable responsibility of married couples and families. They cannot employ methods that fail to respect the person and fundamental human rights, beginning with the right to life of every innocent human being.

This cultural change demands the courage from everyone to adopt a new lifestyle—making practical choices at the personal, family, social, and international level—on the basis of a correct scale of values: *the primacy of "being" over "having."* Other people are not rivals from whom we must defend ourselves, but brothers and sisters to be supported. The mass media has an important role to ensure that the messages that they transmit will support the culture of life.

The Role of Women

Women who have had an abortion should know that the church is aware of how painful and even shattering such a decision is in many cases. Although it is terribly wrong, such women should not give in to discouragement and should not lose hope. They should try to understand what happened and trust in repentance. With expert help, and as a result of one's own painful experience, it is possible to become eloquent defenders of everyone's right to life.

The gospel of life is for the whole of human society. To be actively pro-life is to contribute to the renewal of society through the promotion of the common good. There can be no true peace unless life is defended and promoted. (EV 78, 79, 81, 82, 88-99)

REFLECTION QUESTIONS

1. Why is racism considered to be sinful?

2. What are some indications that racism is still present in your own community today?

3. What steps could be undertaken by a faith community to address the issues of racism in a concrete and constructive way?

4. Why is capital punishment such a controversial issue today?

5. After reading summaries of *The Gospel of Life* and the bishops' statement on capital punishment, have your own thoughts in regard to the death penalty changed at all? Why or why not?

6. Why do the bishops believe that capital punishment does not serve as a strong deterrent to violent crime?

7. How might a parish or local community implement the recommendations made by the bishops for reform and rehabilitation of the present correctional system?

8. Why does John Paul see an urgency to the proclamation of the "gospel of life"?

9. What do you believe are the most serious contemporary threats to life and its respect?

10. What examples can you give of what John Paul II refers to as the "culture of death"?

11. What steps could a parish take to increase awareness of life issues in the parish? The wider community?

12. Do you believe that the church's position concerning the death penalty is consistent with its position on other issues concerning human life? Why or why not?

13. What educational efforts could be made by a parish/social action committee/local community to raise consciousness in regard to the issues raised in *The Gospel of Life*?

14. Which practical recommendations found in *The Gospel of Life* could be implemented in your area?

CHAPTER 2

Call to Family, Community, and Participation

The family is recognized as the basic unit of society, where the values of the social teachings of the church are affirmed and taught. Every government has the responsibility of protecting, supporting, and encouraging the family for the basic well-being of the entire society. This chapter includes summaries from Rerum Novarum *by* Pope Leo XIII, Quadragesimo Anno *by Pope Pius XI, and* Centesimus Annus *and* Evangelium Vitae *by Pope John Paul II.*

THE CONDITION OF LABOR, *RERUM NOVARUM*
POPE LEO XIII

Each Family Possesses Certain Rights

The parents of a family have the obligation, imposed by nature itself, to see that their offspring are provided with all the necessities of life. Families possess the rights, at least equal to civil society, in choosing those things that are necessary for protection and just liberty. Civil power should respect the family and not interfere with its operation unless there is a grave violation of mutual rights within the family itself. (RN 20, 21)

Support for the Worker and Family

The wage paid to the worker must be sufficient for the worker and the worker's family. Reforms are in order when such a wage is not paid. However, it is not just to demand wages that are so high that an employer cannot pay them without financial ruin. Employers and employees should join their efforts to overcome these difficulties and obstacles, aided by the wise measures of the public authority. (QA)

ON THE HUNDREDTH ANNIVERSARY OF
RERUM NOVARUM, CENTESIMUS ANNUS
POPE JOHN PAUL II

"Human Ecology": The Family

The first and fundamental structure of "human ecology" is the family where each individual learns what it means to be a person. It often happens that people are discouraged from creating the proper conditions for human reproduction. Individuals are led to consider themselves and their lives as a series of sensations to be experienced rather than as a work to be accomplished. The result is a lack of freedom, which causes a person to reject a commitment to enter into a stable relationship with another person and to bring children into the world. It leads people to think of children as one of the many "things" which an individual can have or not have, according to taste, and which compete with other possibilities.

It is necessary to see the family as the sanctuary of life. The family is indeed sacred, the place in which life—the gift of

God—can be properly welcomed and protected against the many attacks to which it is exposed. Human ingenuity seems to be directed more toward limiting, suppressing, or destroying the sources of life than toward defending and opening up the possibilities of life.

When economic freedom becomes autonomous and the individual is seen more as a producer or consumer of goods than as a subject who produces and consumes in order to live, then economic freedom loses its necessary relationship to the human person and ends up alienating and oppressing the individual.

The church has no models to present for an effective economic system, since these can only arise within the framework of different historical situations and from the efforts of those responsible with confronting concrete problems. But the church can offer its social teaching as an indispensable and ideal orientation which recognizes the positive value of the market and of enterprise, but points out that at the same time these must be oriented toward the common good. (CA 30-39, 43)

THE GOSPEL OF LIFE, *EVANGELIUM VITAE*
POPE JOHN PAUL II

Role of the Family

The family has a decisive responsibility as the domestic church to proclaim, celebrate, and serve the gospel of life. It celebrates the gospel of life through daily prayer, both individually and as a family. The actual daily life together as a family, as a life of love and self-giving, becomes a service to the gospel of life.

Special attention must also be given to the elderly who must be considered the object of our concern who also have a valuable contribution to make to the gospel of life. The rich treasury of experiences they have acquired through the years are a source of wisdom and witness of hope and love.

Mobilization of Consciences

Urgently needed is a general mobilization of consciences and a united ethical effort to activate a great campaign to support all life. This must begin with the renewal of culture of life within Christian communities themselves. We need to promote a serious and in-depth exchange about basic issues of human life with everyone, including non-believers. The first and fundamental step toward cultural transformation consists in forming consciences with regard to the incomparable and inviolable worth of every human life. There is a need for education about the value of life from its very origin, helping the young to understand and appreciate the experience of sexuality and love and the whole of life according to their true meaning and in their close interconnection. Education is needed for couples concerning true parenthood. Education is also needed concerning the realities of suffering and death. (EV 92-98)

REFLECTION QUESTIONS

1. How does the state hinder/help parents in their parental responsibilities?

2. What are the most serious economic challenges parents (and especially single parents) face today?

3. What most challenges the ability of a family to develop a God-centered family orientation?

CHAPTER 3

Rights and Responsibilities

The church proclaims the right of all to the common good, personal responsibility as well as social rights. It is the responsibility of the state to ensure that the basic rights of each citizen are preserved and defended. The selections included under this topic include Economic Justice for All: Pastoral Letter on Catholic Social Teaching and the U.S. Economy, *issued November 18, 1986, and* Socially Responsible Investment Guidelines, NCCB/USCC, *November 1991.*

ECONOMIC JUSTICE FOR ALL
U.S. BISHOPS

The Church and the U.S. Economy

The United States plays a preeminent role in an interdependent global economy. Nations separated by geography, culture, and ideology are linked in a complexity of financial, technological, and environmental networks. An increasing global interdependence can sometimes be perceived by less developed countries as a pattern of domination.

There exist a number of challenges to the domestic economy, in that the promise of the "American dream"—freedom for all persons to develop their God-given talents in full—remains unfulfilled for many millions in the United States today. Harsh poverty continues to plague the country. The lack of a supportive relation between family life and economic life is one of the most serious problems facing the United States today.

A strong moral vision is needed to face these problems. The fundamental moral criterion for all economic decisions, policies, and institutions must be that they are at the service of all people, especially the poor. (EJFA 10, 13, 16, 18, 24)

The Christian Vision of Economic Life

The basis for all that is believed about the moral dimension of economic life is its vision of the transcendent worth—the sacredness—of human beings, created in the image of God (Gn 1:27). Wherever our economic arrangements fail to conform to the demands of human dignity, they must be questioned and transformed. God has entered into a sacred covenant with humanity through the people of Israel, our forerunners in faith. God is described as a God of justice. The justice of a community is measured by the treatment that is extended to the powerless in society.

Jesus enters into history and proclaims the reign of God, challenging us to seek ways in which God's revelation of the dignity and destiny of all creation might become incarnate in history.

Jesus challenges his followers to a change of heart: to proclaim God's reign and to follow his example in taking the side of those most in need, physically and spiritually. The vision of Jesus challenges the church to see things from the side of the poor and powerless, and to assess lifestyle, policies, and social institutions in terms of their impact upon the poor.

The Christian is a member of a new community of hope, in the new creation of Christ that can reconcile a broken world. The Word made flesh into human history gives strength and hope to overcome injustice. (EJFA 28, 35, 38, 45, 52, 55)

The Various Dimensions of Justice

The virtues of citizenship, which include a sense of one's dependence on the commonwealth, must also guide the economic institutions of society.

Commutative justice calls for a fundamental fairness in all agreements and exchanges between individuals or private social groups. Such a perspective demands respect for the equal dignity of all persons in economic transactions.

Distributive justice requires that the allocation of income, wealth, and power in a society be evaluated in light of its effects on persons whose basic material needs are unmet.

Social justice implies that persons have an obligation to be active and productive participants in the life of society and that society has a duty to enable them to participate in this way.

Christian faith imposes certain limits on how we can view material goods. Americans are challenged today as never before to develop an inner freedom to resist the temptation to seek more.

Positive action is needed, that social and political institutions will be created that will enable all persons to become active members of society.

As individuals and as a nation, we are called to make a fundamental option for the poor and to evaluate social and economic activity from the viewpoint of the poor and the powerless. (EJFA 66, 69-71, 75)

Social Sin

Basic justice demands the establishment of minimum levels of participation in the life of the human community for all persons. Such marginalization, when actively determined by a person, people, or government, can be described as a form of social sin. Respect for human rights and personal and community responsibility are closely linked. A new order must be created that guarantees the minimum conditions of human dignity in the economic sphere for every person.

To address these issues, the active participation of government will be necessary, under the auspices of "subsidiarity."

Governments should undertake only those initiatives that exceed the capacity of individuals or private groups acting independently.

All members of the Christian community are called to a discernment of the hurts and opportunities of the world around them, in order to respond to the pressing needs and thus build up a more just society. (EJFA 77, 79, 81, 87, 124)

Economic Policy Issues

Employment

Full employment is the foundation of a just economy. Employment is a basic right that protects the freedom of all to participate in the economic life of the society. It is a deep conviction of American culture that work is central to the freedom and well-being of people. The nation cannot afford the economic costs, social dislocation, and enormous human tragedies caused by unemployment. Discrimination in employment is one of the causes for high rates of joblessness.

A consensus must be developed that everyone has a right to employment. The burden of securing full employment falls on everyone—policymakers, business, labor, and the general public.

The general economic policies of the government are essential tools for encouraging steady economic growth. (EJFA 69, 141, 147, 153)

Poverty

Poverty is a condition experienced at some time by many people in different walks of life. Many remain poor for extended periods of time.

Most distressing is the number of children that are affected. Many poor families with children receive no government assistance, have no health insurance, and cannot pay medical bills. Due to their mother's lack of access to high quality prenatal care, poor children are disadvantaged even from birth.

There has also been a significant rise in the number of woman in poverty. This has been the result of many factors, including wage discrimination.

Racial minorities are susceptible to poverty, oftentimes due to discrimination. Despite gains that have been made toward racial equality, the effects of past discrimination as well as discrimination in our own time continues to exclude many members of racial minorities from the mainstream of American life.

The economy of the United States is marked by a very uneven distribution of wealth and income. Unequal distribution should be evaluated in terms of several moral principles, including the priority of meeting the basic needs of the poor and increasing the level of participation by all members of society in the economic life of the nation. The most appropriate and fundamental solutions to poverty will be those that enable people to take control of their lives. We must continue to develop sound social welfare programs with a new creativity and commitment.

The search for more human and effective ways to deal with poverty is not limited to short-term reform measures, but rather includes a variety of creative efforts to fashion a system of income support that protects the basic dignity of the poor. (EJFA 174-178, 181, 182, 185, 188, 192, 215)

Food and Agriculture

Many farmers face serious challenges to their economic well-being, including persistent high interest rates. United States international trade policies have also affected the farmer, since past emphasis on producing for oversees markets has contributed to a strain on our natural resource base.

The diversity and richness in American society are being lost as farm people leave the land and as rural communities decay.

The U.S. food system is an integral part of the larger economy of the nation and of the world. There must be a determination that the United States will play an appropriate role in meeting global food needs and a commitment to bequeath to future generations an enhanced natural environment and ready access to the necessities of life. (EJFA 223, 226, 250)

The U.S. Economy and Developing Nations

The demands of Christian love and human solidarity challenge all economic actors to choose community over chaos. Basic justice implies that all peoples are entitled to participate in the increasingly interdependent global economy. Respect for human rights, both political and economic, implies that international decisions must be shaped by values that are more than economic. The special place of the poor means that meeting the basic needs of the millions of deprived and hungry people in the world must be the number one objective of international policy. (EJFA 258)

SOCIALLY RESPONSIBLE INVESTMENT GUIDELINES
NCCB/USCC

Principles for NCCB/USCC Investments

The NCCB/USCC is called to exercise faithful stewardship in managing its financial resources. It draws its values, directions, and criteria from the gospel, universal church teaching, and conference statements. To carry out its mission properly, the conference depends on a reasonable return on investment. Religious mandate and fiscal responsibility suggest a need for clear and comprehensive policies to guide the conference's investments.

The pastoral letter "Economic Justice for All" emphasized three themes related to this topic:

Church as Shareholder and Investor: Individual Christians and those responsible within church institutions who are shareholders must see to it that the invested funds are used responsibly. As part owners, they must cooperate in shaping policies through dialogue with management, voting at corporate meetings, introduction of resolutions, and participation in investment decisions. The bishops support efforts to develop alternate investment policies, especially those that help foster economic development in depressed communities and help the church to respond to local and regional needs.

Shareholder Responsibility: Return on investment is not an adequate rationale for shareholder decisions. Serious, long-term study should be done in relating the rights and responsibilities of shareholders to those of other communities affected by corporate decisions.

Church as Economic Actor: All the moral principles governing the just operation of any economic endeavor apply to the church and its agencies. The church must be exemplary in this regard.

The principles of wise stewardship of financial resources and socially conscious investment criteria are carried out by a consistent strategy. These strategies seek to avoid participation in harmful activities, pursue the good, and use the conference's role as stockholder for social stewardship.

To do no harm refers to a refusal to invest in companies whose products and/or policies are counter to the values of Catholic moral teaching. It may also refer to divesting or refusal to invest based on the principle of cooperation and the avoidance of scandal. In these cases prudence is the guiding principle.

Pursuing the good refers to a positive strategy of seeking to invest in companies that promote values consonant with Catholic social teaching while earning a reasonable rate of return. It also refers to "alternate investments" which may result in a lower rate of return but advance the church's preferential option for the poor or produce some truly significant social good.

Social stewardship refers to a strategy of active corporate participation, actively seeking to influence the corporate culture and to influence corporate policies and decisions.

NCCB/USCC Investment Policies

At the present time the NCCB/USCC investment policies cover the following areas: abortion, contraception, military spending, nuclear armaments, and South Africa.

Abortion: Absolute exclusion of investment in companies whose activities include direct participation in abortion.

Contraceptives: The NCCB/USCC will not invest in companies which manufacture contraceptives.

Military spending: The conference seeks to discourage any nuclear and conventional arms race and to limit the distortion in the U.S. and global economy resulting from disproportionate military spending. It therefore avoids investment in firms primarily engaged in military weapons production or the development of weapons inconsistent with Catholic teaching on war.

South Africa: The NCCB/USCC follows the guidance of the Southern African Catholic Bishops' Conference on economic pressures to dismantle apartheid and joins with others to encourage corporations to act decisively against apartheid.

Also under consideration are policies in regard to affordable housing, racism, sexism, and women's participation in economic life.

REFLECTION QUESTIONS

1. What areas concerning economic justice could be reflected on in your local community?

2. How does the vision of Jesus Christ challenge the church in the area of economic justice?

3. How can a society be said to be committing "social sin"?

4. How can a parish/local community assist in the programs recommended by the bishops in the area of employment? poverty? food and agriculture? U.S economy and developing nations?

5. What should be considered as a rationale for shareholder decisions concerning investment policies?

6. How can Christian investors practice socially conscious stewardship as recommended in the investment policy of the NCCB/USCC?

CHAPTER 4

Option for the
Poor and Vulnerable

Catholic social teaching proclaims that an important dimension of the gospel of Jesus Christ is the respect, dignity, and assistance that are given to the poor and lowly within society, with whom Jesus Christ so intimately identified himself. This concern extends beyond one's own boundaries—to concern for appropriate development in especially disadvantaged areas throughout the world. Included in the documents that address this topic are Mater et Magistra, *John XXIII;* Populorum Progressio, *Paul VI; and* Sollicitudo Rei Socialis, *John Paul II.*

ON CHRISTIANITY AND SOCIAL PROGRESS,
MATER ET MAGISTRA
POPE JOHN XXIII

Jesus Christ has established the Catholic Church as mother and teacher of nations. The teaching of Christ embraces the whole person, soul and body, intellect and will. For two thousand years the church has held aloft the torch of charity through teaching and example. The most notable evidence of the social teaching and action is the encyclical by Leo XIII, *Rerum Novarum*, where questions in regard to workers' conditions were resolved in conformity with Christian principles. (MM 1, 6, 7)

The Encyclical Rerum Novarum

When the encyclical *Rerum Novarum* was written, it was held by many that no connection existed between economic and moral law, whereby those engaged in economic activity need look no further than their own gain. During this era, trade unions in many different countries were sometimes forbidden, sometimes tolerated, and sometimes recognized in private law. Workers labored under conditions where there were dangers to health, moral integrity, and religious faith. The specter of unemployment was ever present. As a consequence, many workers were indignant at the state of affairs and publicly protested.

Pope Leo XIII in his encyclical proclaimed a social message based on the requirements of human nature itself, conforming to the gospel and reason. He taught that the human person cannot be treated as a commodity. Remuneration is not to be thought of in terms of merchandise, but rather according to the laws of justice and equity.

Private property is a natural right possessed by all, which the state must not suppress. The state must as well take interest in the economic activity of its citizens and promote a sufficient supply of material goods. In addition, the state should see to it that labor agreements are entered into according to the norms of justice. Workers and employers should regulate their mutual relations in a spirit of human solidarity.

The encyclical *Quadragesimo Anno* by Pope Pius XI continued many of the themes of *Rerum Novarum*. It confirmed the natural-law character of private property, encouraged partnership arrangements in worker agreements, and pressed for justice in determining wages. Pope Pius XI emphasized that the organization of economic affairs must be conformable to practical morality. Justice and charity, as the principal laws of social life, must govern economic undertakings. Both within individual countries and among nations, there should be established a juridical order with appropriate public and private institutions, inspired by social justice, so that those involved in economic activities can carry out their tasks in conformity with the common good.

In a radio broadcast of June 1, 1941, Pope Pius XII declared that the church had competence to decide whether the bases of a given social system are in accord with the unchangeable order which God has fixed both in the natural order and revelation. (MM 1, 2, 6, 7, 11, 13-15, 18-21, 27, 31-33, 37-39, 42)

Development of the Teachings of Rerum Novarum

Intervention of Public Authority in Economic Life

It is necessary that public authorities take interest to increase the output of goods and to further social progress for the benefit of all citizens. The intervention of public authorities is based on the principle of subsidiarity—that one should not withdraw from individuals and commit to the community what they can accomplish by their own enterprise and industry. Inasmuch as every social activity should prove a help to members of the body social, it should never destroy or absorb them. Precautionary activities by public authorities in the economic field should avoid restricting the freedom of private citizens and increase the basic rights of each individual person. There cannot be a prosperous and well-ordered society unless both private citizens and public authorities work together in economic affairs.

Our times are known for the multiplication of social relationships, a daily more complex interdependence of citizens. This reality is both a symptom and a cause of the growing intervention of public authorities in private life.

People are joining associations to accomplish goals which they cannot achieve alone, including economic, social, cultural, recreational, and political. An advance in social relationships brings numerous services and advantages. At the same time, opportunities for free actions by individuals are restricted within narrower limits.

Advances in social organizations and their objectives must be accompanied by a correct understanding of the common good by public authorities. As relationships multiply binding people together more closely, the commonwealth must keep in mind the freedom of individual citizens and groups of citizens as the state regulates their undertakings.

Concern for the Working Class

It is distressing to see great masses of workers throughout the world who do not receive a just remuneration in wages for their work. Many times these workers live in conditions that are completely out of accord with human dignity.

It also happens in some of these nations that, in contrast with the extreme need of the majority, there exists great and conspicuous wealth.

Moreover, in economically developed countries, it frequently happens that great, or sometimes very great, remuneration is given for the performance of some task of lesser importance or doubtful utility. Meanwhile, the diligent and profitable work that whole classes of hardworking citizens perform receives low payment and one insufficient for the necessities of life.

It must be reaffirmed, once again, that just as remuneration for work cannot be left entirely to unregulated competition, neither may it be decided arbitrarily at the will of the more powerful. The norms of justice and equity should be strictly observed. This requires that workers receive a wage that is sufficient to lead a life worthy of humanity and to fulfill family responsibilities.

In determining this wage, many factors must be considered, including the economic state of the enterprise within which the worker is employed. Although the standards of judgment in this matter are binding everywhere and always, the measure in which they are to be applied cannot be established unless account is taken of the resources on hand.

The economies of various countries continue to evolve rapidly. The strict demand of social justice calls for a corresponding social development. The economic prosperity of any people is to be assessed not so much from the sum total of goods and wealth possessed as from the distribution of goods according to norms of justice, so that everyone in the community can develop and perfect himself or herself.

On a national level, consideration must be given to providing employment for as many workers as possible, to maintaining a balance between wages and prices, and to making accessible the goods and services for a better life to as many persons as possible. At the same time, efforts must be made either to eliminate or keep within bounds the inequalities that exist between different sectors of the economy. Finally, a humane way of existence must be passed on to the next generation.

Justice is to be observed not merely in the distribution of wealth but also in regard to the conditions under which people engaged in productive activity have an opportunity to assume responsibility and to perfect themselves by their efforts. An economic order is considered to be unjust if the organization and structure be such that human dignity of workers is compromised, or their sense of responsibility is weakened, or their freedom of action is removed.

The right of private property is permanently valid. The right of private individuals to act freely in economic affairs is recognized in vain unless these persons are given the opportunity of selecting and using things necessary for the exercise of this right. It is a right which continually draws its force and vigor from the fruitfulness of labor and which is an effective aid in safeguarding the dignity of the human person.

It is not enough to assert that the person has the right of privately possessing goods unless at the same time an effort is made to spread the use of this right through all ranks of the citizenry.

What has been said does not preclude ownership of goods pertaining to production of wealth by states and in other public bodies. The principle of subsidiarity is to be strictly observed.

It has always been taught that in the right of private property, there is rooted a social responsibility. Whoever has received a larger share of blessings must use them, in addition to one's own perfection, for the benefit of others. (MM 52, 53, 55, 56, 60, 62, 65, 67-74, 79, 82, 83, 109, 112, 113, 116, 117, 119)

New Aspects of the Social Question

Readjustment of the Relationship Between Workers and Management

The progress of events and of time makes it increasingly evident that the relationship between workers and management must be readjusted according to the norms of justice and charity. Within the human community, many nations have not made identical progress in economic and social affairs.

Concern for the Agricultural Enterprise

In agriculture, many farmers have abandoned their productive enterprises, which they see as not offering them a more comfortable life. They should be provided with insurance and social security benefits comparable to those in other professions. Agricultural products should be price protected, worked out by economic experts. In rural areas it is fitting that industries be established and common services be developed that are useful in preserving, processing, and transporting farm products. The family farm will be firm and stable only when it yields income sufficient for decent and humane family living.

In rural areas farmers should join together in fellowships especially when the family itself works the farm. It is proper for rural workers to have a sense of solidarity. Toward this end they should set up mutual aid societies and professional associations. But when wishing to make their influence felt, rural workers should refer, as other categories of workers, to the common good.

Concern for Less Economically Advanced Countries

Perhaps the most pressing problem today is the relationship between economically advanced nations and those in the process of development. Nations that have an abundance cannot ignore those nations that are overcome by poverty and hunger, unable to enjoy basic human rights. For wealthier nations to destroy or to waste goods necessary for the lives of people in need runs counter to our obligations in justice and humanity.

Scientific, technical, and financial cooperation must be enlisted in the effort to assist those in need. Efforts should be made to ensure that improved social conditions and economic advancement occur simultaneously in the agricultural, industrial, and various service sectors.

When economically developed countries assist poorer nations, they should exhibit respect for their culture. They should assist without thought of domination, so that these countries will be able to eventually progress economically on their own initiative.

The church continues to assist in these efforts with the proclamation and reaffirmation of the dignity of the human person.

In the question of population growth, particularly in the more economically deprived nations, these problems should not be posed and resolved in a way that promotes means contrary to the dignity of the human person. These questions can only be resolved if economic and social advances preserve and augment the genuine welfare of individual citizens and of human society as a whole. All must regard the life of the human being as sacred, from its moment of conception. It is the important duty of parents to educate their children, who should be raised with a secure faith in the providence of God.

Cooperation and Mutual Assistance Among Nations

Since the relationship between countries is closer today in every region of the world, it is proper that peoples become more and more interdependent. Because states must on occasion complement one another, they must take into account the interests of other nations. It is necessary for commonwealths to cooperate among themselves and provide mutual assistance. Unfortunately, peoples and states have fear of one another. Energies and resources are widely directed toward destruction rather than the advantage of the human family. That mutual faith may develop among leaders and nations, the law of truth and justice must be acknowledged and preserved on all sides. The guiding principles of morality and virtue must be based only on God. (MM 122, 124, 135, 137, 141, 143, 146, 147, 157, 161, 168, 173, 179, 192-194, 200, 202, 204, 207)

Reconstruction of Social Relationships in Truth, Justice, and Love

Role of Religion in Technological and Economic Development

A false opinion is today popularized holding that a sense of religion implanted in individuals by nature is imaginary and inconsistent with this day and age. Whatever the progress in technology and economic life, there can be no justice as long as individuals fail to realize their great individual dignity. Mutual relations among people absolutely require a right ordering of the human conscience in relation to God, the source of all truth, justice, and love. No folly seems more characteristic of our age than the desire to establish a firm and meaningful temporal order but without God, its necessary foundation.

The individual person is the foundation, cause, and end of all social institutions. This principle, the dignity of the human person, must be applied to the systems and methods that the various situations of time or place either suggest or require. It is important that this social teaching of the Catholic Church be widely studied and disseminated. This teaching, which has truth as its guide, justice as its end, and love as its driving force, must also be applied.

The teachings in regard to social matters are put into effect in three stages: first, the actual situation is examined; then the situation is evaluated carefully in relation to these teachings; then it is decided what can and should be done in order that the traditional norms may be adapted to circumstances of time and place. These three steps can be expressed: *observe, judge, and act.* Members of the church are reminded that in fulfilling their duties and pursuing their goals, they do not allow their consciousness of responsibilities to grow cool or neglect the order of the more important goods. (MM 213, 215, 217, 219, 221, 226, 236, 245).

The church has concern for those people who are striving to escape hunger, misery, disease, and ignorance. The Second Vatican Council has propelled the church to put itself in the service of all people. (PP 1)

Universality of the Problem

The extent of poverty is worldwide, and the people who hunger are making urgent appeals for help. Concrete action must be taken to encourage social justice among all nations and to offer less developed nations the means whereby they can further their own progress. (PP 5)

Nature of the Problem

Many are seeking freedom from oppression of any kind, especially from that imposed by lack of subsistence, health care, and fixed employment. They seek freedom from violence to their dignity as human beings and better education: to seek to do more, know more, and have more in order to be more. Most especially this applies to newly developing nations, once subject to a colonial power. While the wealthy continue to enjoy rapid economic growth and development, the poor develop slowly, setting the stage for an increasing imbalance and social conflict. The new technologies of modern civilization can sometimes threaten traditional cultures and values. (PP 6-8, 10)

The Church's Role in Development

The church has attempted continuously to foster human progress. Especially through missionaries, it has sought to bring not only the gospel to nations but has constructed hospitals, schools, and universities as well. Concerted efforts by all are now needed to assist developing nations with a clear vision of all economic, social, cultural, and spiritual aspects. The church offers to the world what is one of its characteristic attributes: a global vision of the person and of the human race.

Development cannot be limited to economic growth. It must be complete and promote every person and the whole person. The vocation of each individual is to develop and fulfill his or her potential. Through Christ, a more complete fulfillment takes place, the highest goal of personal development.

Each person is a part of society and a part of humankind, and this human solidarity imposes a duty for mutual concern for the development of others. All people are called to work for a "new humanism," a more human condition which may be found by embracing the higher values of love and friendship, prayer and contemplation. Such humanism will help overcome oppressive social structures and foster an increased esteem for the dignity of others. (PP 14, 15, 17, 20, 21)

Action That Must Be Undertaken

God intended the earth and all that it contains for the use of every human being and people. All other rights, including property and free commerce, are subordinate to this principle. Private property does not constitute for anyone an absolute and unconditional right. No one is justified in keeping for his or her exclusive use what is not needed, when others lack basic necessities.

While industrialization in the modern world is a necessity for economic growth, it must always be remembered that the economy is at the service of the human being. Work must be seen as the mission of sharing in the creation of the supernatural world.

Urgent reforms are needed and programs must be undertaken that will reduce inequalities, fight discrimination, and free individuals from various types of servitude. Social progress demands growth in literacy, respect for the family, and the promotion of respect for different cultures. Developing nations must be taught to carefully discriminate concerning what is truly necessary and what is being imposed by other nations, which may not always be for their best interests. (PP 22, 23, 25, 33, 34, 36, 40, 41)

A Spirit of Solidarity

It is in the mutual spirit of understanding and friendship among peoples and nations that a common future can be built for the future of the human race. A search must also begin for practical ways for organization and cooperation so that available resources are pooled. This duty is especially the obligation of better-off nations. Such a developing sense of solidarity can properly flow into aid to developing nations, social justice, and the rectification of inequitable trade relations and universal charity.

It is absolutely necessary to begin dialogue among nations so that financial aid is used to its full advantage, and that developing nations no longer risk being overwhelmed by debts whose repayment swallows up the greater part of their gain.

A worldwide collaboration of which a common fund would be created could be both a means and a symbol in assisting the most destitute of the world.

Nations whose industrialization is limited are faced with serious difficulties when they must rely on their exports to balance their economy and to carry out their plans for development. International trade must be humane and just. International agreements should establish general norms for regulating certain prices, guaranteeing certain types of production, and supporting new industries.

There is a duty to welcome others, especially for developed nations to welcome those from less developed areas. Between civilizations as between persons, sincere dialogue creates brotherhood.

To wage war on misery and to struggle against injustice is to promote, along with improved conditions, the human and spiritual progress of all people, and therefore the common good of humanity. (PP 43, 44, 51, 57, 61, 67, 73, 76)

The social concern of the church directed toward the authentic development of the individual and society, respecting all dimensions of the human person, has expressed itself in varied ways. One such means is through papal encyclicals such as *Populorum Progressio* (March 26, 1967) in which Pope Paul VI attempted to apply the teachings of the Second Vatican Council. This encyclical may be seen as a response to the Council's appeal, especially to those who are "poor or in any way afflicted," which are the "joys and hopes, the griefs and anxieties of the followers of Christ" (*Gaudium et Spes*, 1).

The encyclical, in taking up the theme of development, stresses the legitimacy of the church's involvement in this concern, in continuity with previous encyclicals. The ethical and cultural character of the problems connected with development demand comment and concern from the church. Paul VI in this encyclical presented a moral obligation to political leaders and citizens of rich countries to take into account the interdependence of their conduct and the poverty and underdevelopment of many millions of people.

True development cannot consist in the accumulation of wealth if this is to be gained at the expense of the development of the masses and without due consideration of the social, cultural, and spiritual dimensions of the human being.

The question is raised: how can one justify the fact that huge sums of money which could and should be used for increasing the development of peoples are instead used for the enrichment of individuals or groups, or assigned to the increase of stockpiles of weapons, both in developed and undeveloped countries? If "development is the new name for peace," war is the major enemy of the integral development of peoples. (SRS 1, 5, 8-10)

Survey of the Contemporary World

To be squarely faced is the reality of an innumerable multitude of people—children, adults, and the elderly—who are suffering under the intolerable burden of poverty. There is a persistent and widening gap between the areas of the so-called developed North and the developing South. This picture is complex, especially with the differences of culture and values systems between the various population groups.

Also to be examined must be the various economic and social indices of underdevelopment including illiteracy, difficulty or impossibility of obtaining higher education, inability to share in the building of one's own nation, and various forms of exploitation.

Despite notable attempts at progress by the developing nations, some conditions have become worse, as the wealth of the rich increases and the poverty of the poor remains. Among the specific signs of underdevelopment which increasingly affect the developed countries are two in particular: the *housing crisis* and *unemployment*. Millions of people lack adequate housing, experienced universally and due in large measure to the growing phenomenon of urbanization. Also, with the high rate of population growth, the sources of work seem to be shrinking and the opportunities for employment are decreasing rather than increasing.

Another important phenomenon which must be mentioned as indicative of the interdependence between developed and less developed countries is the international debt. The availability of capital to developing nations, although originally welcomed as a possible investment for development projects, must now be reconsidered, since the debtor nations must now export the capital needed for improving their standard of living.

The developing countries, instead of becoming autonomous nations concerned with their own progress, become parts of a machine, cogs on a gigantic wheel due to the influence of the northern hemisphere.

The possibility and willingness to contribute widely and generously to the common good only justifies a leadership role among nations. If a nation closes in upon itself and fails to meet the responsibilities following from its superior position in the community of nations, it would fall short of its clear ethical duty.

The arms trade is equally to blame as a disorder in regard to the fulfillment of true human need. There exists a strange phenomenon: while economic aid and development plans meet with innumerable obstacles, arms circulate with almost total freedom all over the world.

There exists the festering wound that reveals the imbalances of this world in the form of the millions of refugees who have been deprived of home, employment, family, and homeland. Another painful wound in today's world is the phenomenon of terrorism. Christianity forbids seeking solutions by ways of hatred and the murdering of defenseless people.

It is alarming to see governments in many countries launching systematic campaigns against birth, often the result of pressure and financing from abroad, sometimes made as a condition for granting economic aid. This exhibits an absolute lack of respect for the freedom of choice of the parties involved. It is a sign of an erroneous and perverse idea of true development.

Included, however, in a positive assessment of the issues in development is the full awareness among large numbers of men and women of their own dignity and that of every human being. The influence of the *Declaration of Human Rights*, promulgated some forty years ago by the United Nations Organization, has been influential in this regard.

Also, the conviction growing of a radical interdependence and need for solidarity among nations has been helpful. People are recognizing that they are linked together by a common destiny, which is to be constructed together. (SRS 13-19, 22-25)

Authentic Human Development

Development is not a straightforward process, automatic and unlimited. Nor must "superdevelopment" be held as the ideal, which consists of an excessive availability of every kind of material good for the benefit of certain social groups, easily making people slaves of possessions and of immediate gratification. This is the so-called civilization of "consumption" or "consumerism" which involves so much "throwing away" and "waste." As taught by the Second Vatican Council, "to have" does not in itself improve the human person unless it contributes to the maturing and enrichment of that person's human vocation.

One of the greatest injustices in the contemporary world consists precisely in this: that the ones who possess much are relatively few and those who possess almost nothing are many. The evil consists not so much in "having" but rather in possessing without regard for the quality and the ordered hierarchy of the goods one has.

Development must be measured according to the reality and vocation of the human being in its totality, as both body and spirit.

We must commit ourselves more resolutely to the duty that is urgent for everyone today—to work together for the full development of the whole human being and of all people. As we struggle amidst the deficiencies of underdevelopment and superdevelopment we know that one day the corruptible body will put on incorruptibility, the mortal body immortality (1 Cor 15:54).

The obligation to commit oneself to the development of peoples is not just an individual duty and still less an individualistic one. It is an imperative that obliges each and every man and woman as well as societies and nations. The Catholic Church is ready to collaborate with other churches and ecclesial communities in this effort. Such collaboration is a duty of all toward all. Peoples and nations have a right to their own full development that includes economic and social aspects as well as individual cultural identity and openness to the transcendent. Such development must also respect and promote human rights. Development must be achieved in the framework of solidarity and freedom. True development must be based on the love of God and neighbor. (SRS 22, 28-33)

A Theological Reading of Modern Problems

Because of the essentially moral character of development, it is clear that the obstacles to development likewise have a moral character. The main obstacles to development will be overcome only by means of essentially moral decisions.

It is not out of place to speak of "structures of sin," rooted in personal sin, always linked to the concrete acts of the individuals. God has a plan for humanity, which requires from people clear-cut attitudes, which are expressed in actions or omissions toward one's neighbor. This also involves interference in the process of the development of peoples, the delay or slowness of which must be also judged in this light.

Two particular structures, created as a result of the actions and attitudes opposed to the will of God and the good of neighbor, deserve attention: the all-consuming desire for profit and the thirst for power *at all costs*. Not only individuals, but also nations and blocs fall victim to these attitudes of sin.

One would hope that men and women, even those without explicit faith, would be convinced that the obstacles to integral development are not only economic, but rest on profound attitudes which human beings can make into absolute values. For Christians, there is a change of behavior called "conversion," a relationship to God, to the sin committed, to its consequences, and hence to one's neighbor.

There is an emerging sense of interdependence in the world with important moral consequences. When it becomes recognized as a system determining relationships in the world, in all its economic, cultural, political, and religious elements, its response becomes the virtue of "solidarity." This is not a feeling of vague compassion but a firm and persevering determination to commit oneself to the common good because we are really responsible for all. This determination is based on the solid conviction that what is hindering full development is the desire for profit and thirst for power.

There also exists a growing awareness of solidarity among the poor themselves in their efforts to support one another. The church feels called to take a stand beside the poor and to discern the justice of their requests and to help satisfy them.

The same criterion must be applied by analogy to international relationships, with interdependence transformed into solidarity, based on the principle that the goods of creation are meant for all. The stronger and richer nations must have a sense of moral responsibility for the other nations in order that a strong international system may be established, resting on the foundation of the equality of all peoples and on the necessary respect for their legitimate differences.

Solidarity helps us to see the "other"—whether a person, people, or nation—not just as some kind of instrument, but as a neighbor. One's neighbor is not only a human being with his or her rights and a fundamental equality, but the living image of God, redeemed by the blood of Jesus Christ and placed under the permanent action of the Holy Spirit.

The structures of sin can be overcome only through the exercise of the human and Christian solidarity to which the church calls us, which it tirelessly promotes. (SRS 35-40)

Some Particular Guidelines

The church does not have technical solutions to the problem of underdevelopment. The church is an "expert in humanity" which leads it to extend its religious mission to the various fields where men and women search for happiness, in line with their dignity as persons. Whatever affects the dignity of individuals and peoples, such as authentic development, cannot be reduced to a "technical problem." The church offers its first contribution when it proclaims the truth about Christ, about itself, and about humanity, applying this truth to concrete situations. The instrument used for reaching this goal is the church's social doctrine, a formulation that is the result of a careful reflection on the complex realities of human existence in the light of the church's tradition. It attempts to guide human behavior and a commitment to justice.

Highlighted must be the preferential option for the poor, a primacy in the exercise of Christian charity. This preference for the poor and the decisions it inspires must embrace the immense multitudes of the hungry, the needy, the homeless, those without medical care, and above all, those without hope for a better future. Our daily lives, as well as our decisions in the political and economic fields, must be marked by these realities. Likewise, leaders of nations and the heads of international bodies must keep in mind the true human dimension as a priority in development plans.

The characteristic principle of Christian social doctrine is that the goods of the world are originally meant for all. The right to private property is valid and necessary, but it does not nullify the value of this principle.

The motivating concern for the poor must be translated into concrete actions. For example, the international trade system frequently discriminates against the products of the young industries of the developing countries and discourages the producers of raw materials. The world monetary system is marked by excessive fluctuation of exchange rates and interest rates to the detriment of the balance of payments and the debt situation of the poorer countries.

Development also demands a spirit of initiative from the underdeveloped countries. Each must discover and use to the best advantage its own area of freedom. Each developing country should favor the self-affirmation of each citizen and whatever promotes literacy and the basic education, which completes and deepens it as a direct contribution to true development. These nations must identify their own priorities and clearly recognize their own needs.

Some nations will need to increase food production in order to have always available what is needed for subsistence. Other nations need to reform their political institutions in order to replace corrupt, dictatorial, and authoritarian forms of government by democratic and participatory ones.

This can only be accomplished with the collaboration of all—especially the international community in the framework of solidarity, which includes everyone, beginning with the most neglected. (SRS 41-45)

R E F L E C T I O N   Q U E S T I O N S

1. What insights of John XXIII could be kept in mind as more and more aspects of citizens' lives are regulated by the state?

2. What are the particular concerns today that come from those engaged in the agricultural sector? What

solutions as proposed by John XXIII could be considered today?

3. Does the church have a role today in assisting in the economic development for poorer nations? Why or why not? Is foreign aid a good thing?

4. How does the church understand God's intention and humanity's use of the earth's natural resources? What are the consequences of improper stewardship of our natural resources? What steps could a local community take in this regard?

5. How would you assess the progress that has been made in economic development to combat inequality among nations since the document *Populorum Progressio* was issued?

6. What can be a danger to poorer nations in accepting aid from wealthier countries?

7. Why should the church enter into questions regarding the development of peoples?

8. What areas of development do you believe have become worse since the publication of Paul VI's encyclical on development? What hopeful signs do you see?

9. What do you see, in the area of development, as one of the "greatest injustices" in regard to the differences between the rich and poor nations?

10. What are the "structures of sin" which can prevent or delay true development? How can they be overcome?

11. What specific efforts could be made at a parish or local level to overcome these "structures of sin"?

CHAPTER 5

The Dignity of Work and the Rights of Workers

The church proclaims in its teachings on social justice the need to respect employees and their rights to a just wage, decent work, safe working conditions, association, disability protection, security in retirement, and economic initiatives. In these teachings, labor is given priority over capital. The encyclicals that address the topic of labor include the groundbreaking encyclical of Leo XIII, Rerum Novarum; Quadragesimo Anno by Pope Pius XI; and Laborem Exercens and Centesimus Annus by Pope John Paul II.

THE CONDITION OF LABOR, RERUM NOVARUM
POPE LEO XIII

Purpose for Employment

The primary purpose for engaging in work is to procure property for oneself. By placing his energy to work for the sake of an employer, the laborer does so for the means of obtaining a livelihood. It is wrong for employers to set up a system whereby the goods of private individuals are transferred to the community at large, since it takes away from people the right to own property for which they may dispose of their wages. (RN 9)

Distinctiveness of the Human Being

What makes the human being unique is the use of reason. The human may use goods for the achieving of desired ends, using these goods for the best use in the present and in the future. God gave the whole human race the earth to use, and not just certain individuals. It is for institutions of peoples to determine the limits of private possessions, but the earth never ceases from serving the common interests of all. Those lacking resources supply labor and receive compensation. (RN 11, 14)

Proper Order Within Society

The church draws from the gospels the living truths that can be utilized in the right ordering of just relationships between employer and employee. It is consistent with the teachings of the gospel and of the church that the interests of workers be protected as fully as possible. Toward this end, the resources of the state with its laws and authority should be employed within reasonable limits. (RN 24-26)

Rich and Poor Must Not Be Understood as Adversaries

It cannot be taken for granted that one class of society is naturally opposed to another. Each is dependent upon the other, and it is the church which can bring together and unite the rich and the poor by recalling for them their mutual duties, especially those duties that derive from justice. (RN 28, 29)

Duties of the Worker

Included among the duties of the worker is to perform entirely and conscientiously whatever work has been voluntarily and equitably agreed on. It is also expected that the employee will not injure the property or do harm to employers, to refrain from violence. (RN 30)

Duties of Employers

Workers are not to be treated as slaves. Justice demands that workers always be treated with human dignity, since labor, as gainful employment, is an honorable means of supporting life. It is shameful and inhuman to use people as things for gain. It is also important that the spiritual dimension of the person be honored: employers should see to it that employees are free for adequate periods to attend to religious obligations.

Likewise, the employer should make sure that the employee is not alienated from proper care of family. Work should not be such that it threatens the worker's health, or engages the worker in labor that is not suitable for the person's age or sex.

Among the most important duties for employers is to give every worker what is justly due them. Pay schedules should be established in accord with justice, and to defraud anyone of wages justly due is a great crime. (RN 31, 32)

The Church Reminds the Rich of the Gospel Mandate

Jesus Christ is the teacher of the church and reminds both the rich and poor of the values of life, including the immortality of life and the promise of a life yet to come. Only when we have left this life do we truly begin to live. Whether we abound in the riches of this life or lack them is of no importance in relation to eternal happiness. Jesus by his sufferings has wondrously lightened our burdens and shows us the way to eternal glory. Those who are rich in this life have been admonished by the Lord that wealth is of no avail in entering the kingdom of God, and may make it even more difficult to obtain. One day God will call the wealthy to an accountability for their use of the material resources which they have received. (RN 33, 34)

How People Are to Use Their Possessions

Although to own goods privately is a natural right, each person should share of their goods when seeing that someone else is in need. When the demands of necessity have been sufficiently provided for, it is a duty to give to the poor out of that which remains. Whoever has received from the bounty of God a greater share of goods has received them that they might be employed for the benefit of others. (RN 36)

Poverty Is Not a Disgrace

The church teaches that poverty is not a disgrace and no one should be ashamed because of the labor performed. True dignity is established not by wealth accumulated, but rather by virtue obtained, equitably available to all classes of people, whether poor or rich. God seems to incline more toward the unfortunate since Jesus called the poor to be blessed, embracing with special love the lowly and those harassed by injustice. We should reflect on those things which unite us. All people share in a commonality, since all people have been equally redeemed by the blood of Christ. (RN 37, 38)

The Church Must Tend to Worldly Matters as Well as the Divine

The church teaches concerning virtue that people may realize and implement teachings that will assist in the proper understanding of material existence. By its teaching, the church restrains the twin plagues of life: excessive desire for wealth and thirst for pleasure. The church has traditionally instituted works of charity to assist especially the working class in some of their material need. Many religious organizations and societies have been founded and sponsored by the church that the variety of human ills could be properly cared for. (RN 42-44)

The State Must Provide Aid When Needed

Those governing the state have the responsibility to ensure the well-being of the entire commonwealth, including the workers. Public authority should show proper concern for the worker so that what the worker contributes to the common good may be returned, that each laborer may be housed, clothed and secure, living without hardship.

Since the power of governing comes from God and is a participation in God's sovereignty, it should be administered according to the example of Divine power, which looks to the well-being of individuals and to that of all creation. (RN 51, 52)

Peace and Good Order Needed for the State

It is vitally important for the public welfare and the private good as well that there be peace and good order in the state. The state within limits ought to be free to intervene if disorder is threatened due to strikes or concentrated stoppages of work, or if any threat exists to the integrity of the workers such as practice of their religion and protection of family values. The worker should be free from unjust burdens or anything which would degrade them. Intervention by the state, especially by use of law, should be appropriate and not go further than the remedy requires. (RN 53)

Protection of Rights by the State

Rights must be religiously protected, but most especially the rights of private individuals with special consideration of the poor and the vulnerable within society. Justice does not forbid us from striving for better things, but it does preclude us from taking from another what properly belongs to that individual.

The state should insure that situations that lead to labor strikes—including work that is too long and hard with inadequate pay—are remedied. Such disruptions can inflict damage upon both the employer and the employee, making it well within the interests of the state to anticipate and prevent, by removing the causes.

The power of the state should also protect the goods of the worker's soul, which bears the image and likeness of God. For this reason, it is important that workers be given the opportunity to practice their religion and worship, keeping holy the Sabbath day.

The state should protect the worker from labor that is excessive, extracted merely for the benefit of the employer's greed. Working conditions should be such that rest is provided and that proper safeguards be employed regarding the employment of women and children. Proper time for days off and vacation should be provided, that energy may be restored after labor has been expended. (RN 56-60)

Payment of Wages

It has been taught that free consent fixes the amount of a wage between employer and employee. But underlying such an agreement must be natural justice. It is in the interest of the employer and society that the worker be given a sufficiently large wage to provide comfortably for the worker and the worker's family. Thus a just wage, plus the right to private property, can reasonably insure against violence or public disorder. It is also important that crushing taxes imposed by the state do not drain private wealth away. (RN 65-67).

Workers' Associations

Employers and employees, uniting in institutions and agencies to assist the poor, can accomplish much. It can also be opportune for workers to organize into associations. Such private associations can provide a forum where the worker may be better enabled to assure benefits from the toil expended, but to assure adequate retirement benefits for the future. The state should foster such associations that seek to secure, as far as possible, an increase for the workers in the goods of body, soul, and prosperity. Christian workers should also see to it that associations are formed that provide opportunities for growth in holiness and the Christian life. (RN 74, 75)

ON RECONSTRUCTING THE SOCIAL ORDER,
QUADRAGESIMO ANNO
POPE PIUS XI

Partnership Between Employer and Employee

The wage-contract between employer and worker should be modified when possible by a contract of partnership, in which wage earners are made sharers in some way of the ownership, or the management, or the profits.

Individual and Social Character of Labor

Human society must form a social and organic body, where labor is protected in the social and juridical order and where various forms of human endeavor are united in mutual harmony and mutual support. Brains, capital, and labor must combine for common effort or labor cannot produce due fruit.

The wage scale should be regulated with a view toward the economic welfare of the whole people and the common good. Opportunities need to be provided for those who are willing and able to work. To lower or raise wages unduly, with a view toward private profit and disregard for the common good, is contrary to social justice. By union of effort and good will, a scale of wages should be established which offers the greatest number of opportunities for employment and for securing a suitable means of livelihood.

Subsidiarity

Due to the change in social conditions, much that was formerly done by small bodies can now be done only by large corporations. Just as it is wrong to withdraw from the individual and commit to the community at large what private enterprise and industry can accomplish, so too is it an injustice for a larger and higher organization to arrogate to itself functions which can be performed efficiently by smaller and lower bodies.

The primary responsibility of the state and of all good citizens is to abolish conflict between classes with divergent interests and thus foster and promote harmony between the various ranks of society.

The Dignity of Labor and the Laborer

New questions and concerns are always arising concerning labor and the worker, providing fresh hopes but also fears connected with this basic dimension of human existence. With new developments in technology, the economy, and politics, it is always important for the church to call attention to the dignity and rights of all who work and to call attention to those situations in which the dignity and rights of those who work are violated. (LE 1)

The Individual and Work

The church is convinced that work is a fundamental part of the individual's existence on earth, but sees each human being in the context of the eternal designs and transcendent destiny which has been bestowed by God. As described in the book of Genesis, each and every individual takes part in the giant process of building the earth through labor.

As a person, each individual as the "image of God" is capable of acting in a planned and rational way, directed toward self-realization. However true it is that the person is destined for work and called to it, work is for the person and not the person for the work. (LE 6)

A Right Order of Values

The worker should never be seen solely as an instrument of production. Errors can occur when the individual is treated on the same level as a means of production and not in accordance with the true dignity of the laborer's work. (LE 7)

Worker Solidarity

The reaction against the degradation of the person as the subject of work and exploitation in the area of wages, working conditions, and social security led in the past to worker solidarity and various methods of associating. Great strides and advances have been made by such cooperative efforts. Regretfully, various ideological or power systems have sometimes thwarted these efforts and have allowed flagrant injustices to continue. There must continue, therefore, the study of work and living conditions of workers. New means of creating solidarity among workers must be promoted whenever there is a degradation or exploitation of the worker. The church commits itself to this cause as its mission and service, in order that the dignity of human work will not be violated. (LE 8)

Labor and Personal Dignity

Work is a universal calling and is good for the human person. Through work, the person not only transforms nature, but also achieves fulfillment as a human being, and to a certain extent becomes even more a human being. Work is also the foundation of family life, making it possible to form family since it requires some means of subsistence. Work also influences the process of education in the family.

Each individual also belongs to a greater family, that of the great society, to which the person is joined by particular cultural and historical links. This link allows each person to combine a deep human identity with membership in a nation thereby identifying the individual's labor with the common good of the entire society. (LE 10)

The Priority of Labor Over Capital

The church has always taught the principle of the priority of labor over capital. The concept of capital includes the whole collection of means by which the individual appropriates natural resources and transforms them in accordance with the person's needs. All these means are the result of the historical heritage of human labor. Everything that is at the service of work, including modern technology, is itself the result of work. Therefore, the church stresses always the primacy of persons over things. Capital can never be separated from labor. Always to be avoided is the error of materialism, the conviction of the primacy and importance of the material, which directly or indirectly places the spiritual in a position of inferiority and subordination. (LE 12, 13)

Work and Ownership

Christian tradition has never upheld an absolute or untouchable claim to private ownership. It has always understood this right within the broader context of the right for all to use the goods of the whole of creation, that goods are meant for everyone. The position of "rigid" capitalism, which defends the exclusive right to private ownership of the means of production as an untouchable dogma of economic life, is not acceptable. From this conviction has come forth many proposals from the church, including joint ownership of the means of work, sharing by workers in the management and/or profits of businesses, so-called shareholding by labor, etc. The principle of the priority of labor over capital is an important principle of social morality. The laborer needs not only recompense for work performed, but also needs to know that the labor performed does not make the worker just "a cog in the wheel." Work involves not only the economy, but also, and especially, personal values. (LE 14, 15)

Rights of Workers

The rights of workers must be examined within the broad context of human rights. Such rights, specifically the rights of workers, flow from fundamental obligations including the duty to work which the Creator has commanded, and the human condition which requires work in order to be maintained and developed.

Involved in employment are "indirect employers," i.e., all the agents at the national and international level responsible for the whole orientation of labor policy. Respect for the objective rights of the worker—every kind of worker: manual or intellectual, industrial or agricultural, etc.—must constitute the fundamental criterion for shaping the whole economy. The fundamental issue of providing suitable employment for all who are capable of it needs always to be addressed. It is particularly painful when the young who after technical and professional preparation fail to find work. To meet the dangers of unemployment these agents need to make provision for overall planning, organizing work in a correct and rational way, matched by a suitable system of instructing and education. Thus not only will mature human beings be developed, but at the same time, people will be prepared for the world of work.

The justice of a socioeconomic system can be evaluated by examining whether or not the worker's labor is properly remunerated. Wages are the practical means by which the vast majority of people have access to those goods intended for the common good. Just remuneration for the work of an adult responsible for a family means a wage that properly maintains the family and provides security for its future. Women who desire to join the workforce must not be discriminated against and must not be excluded from jobs for which they are capable. Their family aspirations must likewise be respected, especially their role as mothers.

Various social benefits should be accorded to workers, including medical assistance, health care, vacation time and days off, pension and insurance for old age and accidents at work. Also of importance is the right to a working environment that is safe both physically and morally understood.

Workers also enjoy the right of association, by which they may participate in labor unions where the interests of workers are protected. Just efforts, however, to secure the rights of workers who are united by the same profession should take into account the limitations imposed by the general economic situation of the country. Care should be taken that such unions not "play politics" in the sense that they be subject to the decisions of political parties. Rather, their efforts can profitably be directed toward education and training efforts for workers.

The use of strikes or work stoppages must never be abused, especially for political purposes. When essential community services are in question, means may be needed on behalf of the common good, including appropriate legislation.

Also to be remembered is the importance of agricultural work, which provides society with the goods needed for daily sustenance. In many situations, radical changes are needed to restore to agriculture and to rural people their just value as the basis for a healthy economy.

It must likewise not be forgotten that disabled people deserve consideration in their quest to participate in all aspects of society, including in the work force. Disabled people should be offered the opportunity to work according to their capabilities.

Emigrants, whether in a permanent situation or as a seasonal worker, should not be placed at a disadvantage in comparison with other workers in that society in the matter of working rights. Emigrants in search of work must never become an opportunity for financial or social exploitation. (LE 16-23).

A Spirituality of Work

The word of God contains the truth that the individual created in the image of God shares by his or her work in the activity of the Creator. The Book of Genesis is in a certain sense the first "gospel of work," proclaiming that the human should imitate God the Creator in working, because the human being alone has the unique characteristic of likeness to God. Each person should also imitate God's creative activity under the form of work and rest. Christians are convinced that the triumphs of the human race are a sign of God's greatness and a mysterious unfolding of God's divine plan. By means of work, men and women share in this great work of creation.

Jesus Christ gives eloquent example to the place of work in the Christian life, as a man of work, a craftsman, a member of the working world. He appreciated and respected human work. Sweat and toil, which work necessarily involves in the present condition of the human race, presents the Christian and everyone called to follow Christ with the possibility of sharing in the work that Christ came to do. (LE 24-27)

Toward the "New Things" of Today

Pope Leo XIII, in his encyclical *Rerum Novarum*, which addressed "New Things" of his day, especially in terms of the Industrial Age, predicted that the social order proposed by "socialism" would be a danger to the masses and a radical solution to the "question of the working class" of the time.

The Error of Socialism

The fundamental error of socialism is the consideration of the individual person as an element within the social organism, so that the good of the individual is completely subordinated to the functioning of the socio-economic mechanism. It likewise maintains that the good of the individual can be realized without reference to the person's free choice. This makes it difficult for the person to recognize his or her dignity as a person and hinders progress toward the building of an authentic human community.

The first cause of the mistaken concept of the nature of the person is atheism. The denial of God deprives the individual of his or her foundation and leads to a reorganization of the social order without reference to the person's dignity and responsibility. Socialism derives its choice of the means of action from class struggle, a philosophy condemned in *Rerum Novarum*. Especially condemned was the idea that conflict should not be restrained by ethical or juridical considerations, or by the respect for the dignity of others. What is pursued is not the general good of society but a partisan interest, which replaces the common good and sets out to destroy whatever stands in its way.

Rerum Novarum is opposed to the state control of the means of production, which could reduce every citizen to being a "cog" in the state machine. This encyclical pointed the way to just reforms, which would restore dignity to the work and the worker. It proposed that society and the state assume responsibility for protecting the worker from unemployment by economic policies aimed at ensuring balanced growth and full employment or through unemployment insurance and retraining programs. In addition, the role of trade unions in negotiating minimum salaries and working conditions is decisive. Humane working hours and adequate free time need to be guaranteed.

The Use of "Subsidiarity" by the State to Promote Reform

The state must contribute to the achievement of these goals both directly and indirectly by the principle of *subsidiarity*. It must create conditions for the free exercise of economic activity, defend the weakest, place certain limits on the autonomy of the parties who determine working conditions, and ensure the necessary minimum support for the unemployed worker. Many such reforms were carried out by the state, but the role of the workers' movement was an important contributor.

Rerum Novarum, within the context of the whole magisterium of Leo XIII, points to the consequences of the error of misunderstanding human freedom in which it is detached from obedience to the truth and consequently from the duty to respect the rights of others. (CA 12-17)

Private Property and the Purpose of Material Goods

The church has always defended the right to private property, fundamental for the autonomy and development of the person. At the same time, the church teaches that the possession of material goods is not an absolute right and that its limits are inscribed in its very nature as a human right. Each person should use his or her material possessions as common to all.

The Gift of Work and Land

God gave the earth to humanity so that it might provide sustenance for all without excluding or favoring anyone. This is the foundation of the universal destination of the earth's goods. It is through work that the individual, using intelligence and freedom, makes part of the earth his or her own, the origin of individual property. These two factors—*work* and *land*—are to be found at the beginning of every human society. In our time, the role of human work is becoming increasingly important as the productive factor both of non-material and material wealth. More than ever, work is work with others and work for others.

A new form of ownership has evolved in the form of the possession of know-how, technology, and skill. The ability to foresee both the needs of others and the combination of productive factors most adapted to satisfying those needs constitutes an important source of wealth in modern society. The role of disciplined and creative human work, initiative, and entrepreneurial ability becomes increasingly evident and decisive.

The Poor and the Modern Business Economy

The modern business economy has positive aspects. But it must also be pointed out that many people, perhaps the majority today, do not have the means which would enable them to take their place in an effective and humanly dignified way within a productive system in which work is truly central. They have no way of acquiring the basic knowledge which would enable them to express their creativity and develop their potential. If not actually exploited, they are to a great extent marginalized. Aspects of the Third World also appear in the developed countries, where the constant transformation of the methods of production and consumption devalues certain acquired skills and professional expertise. Those who fail to keep up with the times can easily be marginalized, as can the elderly, the young people who are incapable of finding their place in the life of society, and, in general, those who are weakest. In the Third World context, certain objectives stated by *Rerum Novarum* remain valid, including a sufficient wage for the support of the family, social insurance for old age and unemployment, and adequate protection for the conditions of employment.

There is a wide range of opportunities for commitment and effort in the name of justice on the part of trade unions and other workers' organizations. They defend workers' rights and enable workers to participate more fully and honorably in the life of their nation.

It is right to speak of a struggle against an economic system understood as a method of upholding the absolute predominance of capital, the possession of the means of production and of the land, in contrast to the free and personal nature of human work. In the struggle against such a system, what is being proposed is a society of free work, of enterprise, and of participation. Such a society demands that the market be appropriately controlled by the forces of society and by the state, so as to guarantee that the basic needs of the whole of society are satisfied.

The Role of Profit in Business

The church acknowledges the legitimate role of profit as an indication that a business is functioning well. But profitability is not the only indicator of a firm's condition. It is possible for a firm's financial accounts to be in order and yet for the people—who make up the firm's most valuable asset—to be humiliated and their dignity offended. The purpose of a business firm is not simply to make a profit, but in its existence as a community of persons who are endeavoring to satisfy their basic needs and who form a particular group at the service of the whole of society.

Relations Between Poor and Wealthy Nations

Stronger nations must offer weaker ones opportunities for taking their place in international life. It is not right for the wealthier nations to expect payment of debts from the poorer nations when the effect would be the imposition of political choices leading to hunger and despair for entire peoples. It cannot be expected that the debts contracted should be paid at the price of unbearable sacrifices. In such cases it is necessary to find ways to lighten, defer, or even cancel the debt that is compatible with the fundamental right of peoples to subsistence and progress.

The Danger of Consumerism

Included among threats and problems emerging within the more advanced economies must be included the phenomenon of consumerism. In singling out new needs and new means to meet them, one must be guided by a comprehensive picture of the human being, which respects all the dimensions of the person and subordinates material and instinctive dimensions to interior and spiritual ones. If, on the contrary, a direct appeal is made to instincts while ignoring the reality of the person as intelligent and free, then consumer attitudes and lifestyles can be created which are objectively improper and often damaging to the person's physical and spiritual health. A great deal of educational and cultural work is needed, including the education of consumers in the responsible use of their power of choice, the formation of a strong sense of responsibility among producers and among people in the mass media in particular, as well as the necessary intervention by public authorities.

A striking example of artificial consumption is the use of drugs. Widespread drug use is a sign of a serious malfunction in the social system; it also implies a materialistic, and in a certain sense, a destructive "reading" of human needs.

It is not wrong to want to live better; what is wrong is a style of life which is presumed to be better when it is directed toward "having" rather than "being," which wants to have more, not in order to be more but in order to spend life in enjoyment as an end in itself.

Respect for the Earth and Environment

Equally worrisome is the ecological question. In the desire to have rather than to be and to grow, humanity consumes the resources of the earth in an excessive and disordered way. Humanity believes it can make arbitrary use of the earth without regard to its original, God-given purpose. Humanity must be conscious of its duties and obligations toward future generations.

Humanity must likewise be conscious of serious destruction that takes place to the human environment. There exist serious problems in modern urbanization. Each individual is conditioned, to a certain extent, by the social structure, by education received, and by the environment. These elements can either help or hinder the individual in living in accordance with the truth.

When economic freedom becomes autonomous and the individual is seen more as a producer or consumer of goods than as a subject who produces and consumes in order to live, then economic freedom loses its necessary relationship to the human person and ends up alienating and oppressing the individual.

The church has no models to present for an effective economic system, since these can only arise within the framework of different historical situations and from the efforts of those responsible with confronting concrete problems. But the church can offer its social teaching as an indispensable and ideal orientation which recognizes the positive value of the market and of enterprise, but points out that at the same time these must be oriented toward the common good. (CA 30-39, 43)

State and Culture

Pope Leo XIII was aware of the need for a sound theory of the state to ensure the normal development of the human being's spiritual and temporal activities. He presented the organization of society according to the three powers: legislative, executive, and judicial, a concept commonly understood in secular government but a novelty in church teaching. This is the principle of the "rule of law" in which law is sovereign, not the arbitrary will of individuals.

The church values the democratic system inasmuch as it ensures the participation of citizens in making political choices, and provides the possibility of electing and holding accountable those who govern them and of replacing them through peaceful means when appropriate.

The Development of Authentic Democracy

Authentic democracy is possible only in a state ruled by law, and on the basis of a correct conception of the human person. Those who are convinced they know the truth and firmly adhere to it are considered unreliable from a democratic point of view, since they do not accept that the majority determines truth, or that it is subject to variation according to different political trends. However, if there is no ultimate truth to guide and direct political activity, then ideas and convictions can easily be manipulated for reasons of power. History shows that a democracy without values easily turns into open or thinly disguised totalitarianism.

The church is also aware of the dangers of fanaticism and fundamentalism when some attempt to impose in the name of an ideology their own concept of what is true and good. Christian truth is not an ideology and recognizes that human life is realized in history in conditions that are diverse and imperfect. In reaffirming the dignity of the person, the church's method is respect for freedom. But freedom attains its full development only by accepting the truth. In a world without truth, freedom loses its foundation.

In the flowering of democratic ideals in nations formally under a totalitarian regime, it is important that recognition be given to certain explicit rights, including: the right of the child to develop in the mother's womb from the moment of conception, the right to live in a united family and in a moral environment, the right to develop one's intelligence and freedom in seeking and knowing the truth, the right to share in the work which makes wise use of the earth's material resources, and the means to support one's self and family and to have and to rear children. The source of such freedoms is religious freedom, the right to live in the truth of one's faith. The contribution of the church to the political order is its vision of the dignity of the person revealed in all the mystery of the Incarnate Word.

The Economic Activity of the State

The economic activity of the state also presupposes sure guarantees of individual freedom and private property, as well as stable currency and efficient public services. The principle task of the state is to guarantee this security, so that those who work and produce can enjoy the fruits of their labor, and feel encouraged to work efficiently and honestly.

Another task is overseeing and directing the exercise of human rights in the economic sector. The state has a duty to sustain business activities by creating job opportunities.

Care must be taken in terms of abuses in the assistance provided by the state to those who need remedies for poverty and deprivation. The principle of subsidiarity must be respected: a community of a higher order should not interfere in the internal life of a community of a lower order. By intervening directly and depriving society of its responsibility, the social assistance state leads to a loss of human energies and an inordinate increase of public agencies.

Faithful to the mission received from Christ, the church has always been present and active among the needy, offering them material assistance in ways that neither humiliate nor reduce them to mere objects of assistance.

In order to overcome today's widespread individualistic mentality, there is required a concrete commitment to solidarity and service, beginning in the family. Evangelization also plays a role in the various nations, directed now at culture itself, so that culture is sustained in its progress toward the truth, assisting in the work of its purification and enrichment.

The church promotes those aspects of human behavior which favor a true culture of peace, as opposed to models in which the individual is lost in the crowd, in which the role of his or her initiative and freedom is neglected. (CA 44, 46-51)

The Person as the Way of the Church

The church is addressing the concrete individual human being, included in the mystery of redemption. This concern is the principle which inspires the church's social doctrine, which has been developed in a systematic way especially throughout the last century.

The church's social doctrine focuses on the human being as an individual involved in a complex network of social relationships. But the true identity of each individual is known only through faith. This social doctrine is an instrument of evangelization, proclaiming God and the mystery of salvation in Christ to every human being. Because its activity today meets with particular difficulties and obstacles, the church devotes itself to new energies and new methods of evangelization to ensure the safeguarding of the transcendence of the human person.

Love for others and love for the poor especially is made concrete in the promotion of justice. It is not enough to draw on surplus goods for the sake of the poor, but also a change of lifestyle is needed, encouraging new models of production and consumption. (CA 53-55, 58)

REFLECTION QUESTIONS

1. Does the church have a role to play in teaching about labor relations? Why or why not?

2. How have the roles of employer and employee changed since the time of Leo XIII? Does this necessitate a change in the teachings in this regard?

3. What do you believe are the advantages of labor associations for the worker? For the employer? Disadvantages for both? Has the role of associations and unions changed over the years? For better or worse?

4. Are the criteria for a just wage proposed by Pius XI still workable guidelines? Why or why not?

5. What cautions should be considered by workers who would utilize work stoppages or strikes?

6. What resources could be made available at a parish, regional, or diocesan level to assist those who are presently unemployed and searching for work or in need of temporary assistance?

7. How could John Paul II's vision of a "spirituality of work" be incorporated into the contemporary work force?

8. Should "profitability" be considered the only criterion to be used as a gauge of business success? If not, what other criteria could be used?

9. What are the most serious dangers posed by consumerism to developed countries?

10. How can Christians work to change the "consumer mentality" that affects so much of society today?

CHAPTER 6

Solidarity

The church teaches a basic solidarity among all citizens and a responsibility to work together for the benefit of all. There is a call from the gospels to live in harmony and peace based on just principles that include a respect for each human person and their own unique cultural roots and ethnicity, which should extend as well to respect for other nations and cultures. The following summaries are taken from the encyclical Pacem in Terris, by Pope John XXIII; and The Challenge of Peace: God's Promise and Our Response, by the U.S. bishops.

> PEACE ON EARTH, *PACEM IN TERRIS*
> POPE JOHN XXIII

Order in the Universe

Peace on earth can be firmly established only if the order laid down by God can be observed by humanity. So, too, for each person there is written in the heart an order revealed by the conscience. There are laws within the nature of humanity written by God, which can help states in their relationships with each other. (PT 1, 5, 7)

Order Between Persons

Every human being is a person with a nature endowed with intelligence and free will. Every human being has rights and obligations, which flow directly from personhood. (PT 9, 10)

Rights

Each person has a right to life, to bodily integrity and the means suitable for the proper development of life, primarily food, clothing, shelter, rest, medical care, and necessary social services.

There are several rights given to each person in virtue of natural law which pertain to moral and cultural values: a good reputation, freedom in searching for truth and expressing and communicating opinions, the pursuit of art within the limits laid down by the moral order and common good. There is also the right to be informed truthfully about public events.

The natural law also provides the right to share in the benefits of culture and basic education; the right to worship according to the dictates of one's conscience and to practice religion privately and publicly. One also has the right to choose freely the state of one's life, the right to establish a family, with equal rights and duties for men and women. Parents have the right to support and education of their children.

Individuals have the right to an opportunity to work and good working conditions; women have the right to working conditions consonant with their duties as wives and mothers. There exists the natural right to carry on economic activities and to a wage determined by the criterion of justice and in keeping with the dignity of the human person. There is also the right to private property.

From the fact that human beings are social comes the right of assembly and association. There exists the right to freedom of movement, within one's country and to emigrate when there are just reasons. There is a right to participate in political affairs and to contribute to the common good. There is also a right to juridical protection of rights according to the norm of law. (PT 11-21, 23-27)

Duties

The natural rights are inseparably connected with respective duties. A well ordered society demands that each person recognize and observe one another's mutual rights and duties.

The order which prevails in society is by nature moral and grounded in the truth, and must function according to the norms of justice, inspired and perfected by mutual love and brought to balance in freedom.

There are three characteristics of the present day: first, working classes have gained ground in economic and public life. Second, women are taking more of a role in public life as they become more and more conscious of their Christian dignity. Third, the world human society has taken on a new appearance in the field of social and political life. (PT 28, 31, 39-42)

Relations Between Individuals and the Public Authorities

Human society must have some people invested with legitimate authority to preserve its institutions and to devote themselves to care and work for the good of all. These individuals derive their authority from God. Their power to command comes from the moral order, which has God as its Creator and final end.

Civil authority must appeal to the conscience of the individual citizen. If civil authorities pass laws or command anything opposed to the moral order and therefore contrary to the will of God, neither the laws made nor the authorizations granted can be binding on the conscience of the citizens.

Individual citizens are obliged to make their specific contribution to the common welfare. The ethnic characteristics of the various human groups are to be respected as constituent elements of the common good. The very nature of the common good requires that all members of the state be entitled to share in it, although in different ways according to one's tasks, merits, and circumstances. Those in public authority must give more attention to the less fortunate members of the community since they are less able to defend themselves. Civil authorities should promote simultaneously the spiritual and material welfare of the citizens. To safeguard the inviolable rights of the human person and to facilitate the fulfillment of each person's duties should be the chief duty of every public authority. It is necessary that the administration give wholehearted and careful attention to the social as well as to the economic progress of the citizens.

The common good requires that civil authorities maintain a careful balance between coordinating and protecting the rights of the citizens on the one hand, and promoting them on the other. It is in keeping with the innate demands of human nature that the state should take a form that embodies the three-fold division of powers.

The people of our time are becoming increasingly conscious of their dignity as human persons. It is required that government officials be chosen in conformity with constitutional procedures and perform their specific functions within the limits of law. (PT 46-48, 51, 53, 55-58, 60, 64, 65, 68, 79)

Relations Between States

Nations are reciprocally subjects of rights and duties, and their relationships must also be harmonized in truth, in justice, in working solidarity, and in liberty. The same natural law that governs relations between individual human beings also serves to regulate relations of nations with one another. Authority cannot thwart the moral order, lest it sweep aside its very foundation. A fundamental factor of the common good is the acknowledgment of the moral order.

The first rule governing the relations between states is that of *truth*. All nations must be recognized to be equal in dignity. Each nation is invested with the right to existence, to self-development, to the means fitting to its attainment, and to be the one primarily responsible for its self-development. It also has the right to a good name and the respect that is its due.

Relations between nations are further regulated by *justice*. Nations are bound by the obligation to effectively guard each of their rights and to avoid actions that may jeopardize them. Disagreements between nations should be resolved by a mutual assessment of the reasons for both sides of the dispute and by a mature and objective investigation and equitable reconciliation of the differences of opinion.

Justice is violated by whatever is done to limit the strength and numerical increase of people of the same ethnic group within a country. Civil authorities should take means to improve the lot of the citizens of an ethnic minority. Ethnic minorities should also make efforts to associate with the larger cultural milieu and share in their customs and institutions. The universal common good requires that in every nation friendly relations be fostered in all fields between the citizens and their intermediate societies.

It is approved and commended that every charitable effort be made to make migration of person from one country to another less painful.

Justice and right reason demands that the arms race among nations should cease and that the parties concerned should reduce the stockpile of weapons that exist in various countries equally and simultaneously. Nuclear weapons should be banned, and all should come to an agreement on a fitting program of disarmament, employing mutual and effective controls.

Relations between states should be based on freedom; no country may unjustly oppress another or unduly meddle in another's affairs. It is vitally important that the wealthier states, in providing forms of assistance to the poorer, should respect the moral values and ethnic characteristics peculiar to each and avoid any intention of political domination.

It is hoped that by meeting and negotiating, people may come to discover better the bonds that unite them together, deriving from their human nature, which indeed bind them together. It is not fear but love that should reign, expressing itself in collaboration. (PT 80, 83, 85, 86, 91-95, 97, 100, 107, 112, 120, 125, 129)

Relationship of People and Political Communities

The progress of science and technology has profoundly influenced human conduct and advanced the opportunity for cooperation and association with one another. The interdependence of world economies has grown deeper. The social progress, order, security, and peace of each country are necessarily connected with the social progress, order, security, and peace of all other countries. Individual countries cannot rightly seek their own interests and develop themselves in isolation from the rest.

Under the present circumstances of human society, no one nation or several nations can be considered adequate to promote the universal common good. The moral order would require that some form of public authority be established that would have worldwide power and be endowed with the proper means for the efficacious pursuit of its objective, the universal common good in concrete form. It must be set up by common accord and not imposed by force. This public and universal authority must have for its objective the recognition, respect, safeguarding, and promotion of the rights of the human person.

The relationships that exist between the worldwide public authority and the public authorities of individual nations must be governed by the principle of *subsidiarity*, allowing the public authorities to carry out their tasks and duties and exercise their rights with greater security.

It is hoped that the United Nations Organization, established in 1945, may become ever more equal to the magnitude and nobility of its task of maintaining and consolidating peace between peoples. (PT 130, 135, 138, 139, 141, 142, 145)

Pastoral Exhortations

Christians should endeavor, in the light of faith and with the strength of love, to ensure that the various economic, social, cultural, or political institutions facilitate human beings perfecting themselves in the natural and supernatural order.

It is necessary that human beings should live and act in their temporal lives to create a synthesis between scientific, technical, and professional elements on the one hand and spiritual values on the other. In the temporal activity, *faith* should be present as a beacon that gives light, and *charity* should be present as a force to give life.

An integral education is needed for our young, combining religious values and moral conscience formation with the assimilation of scientific and technical knowledge.

Constant endeavors must be made to objectify the criterion of justice with the reality of concrete situations, marked in these days with continuous dynamism.

Opportunity is ever unfolding for cooperation between Christians from different traditions as well as with those with no Christian faith at all, in a myriad of social and economic affairs. Every believer in this world must be a spark of light, a center of love and a vivifying leaven in society, bringing about true peace in the order established by God. There can be no peace among people unless there is peace in each person. (PT 146, 150, 152-155, 158, 163-165)

> THE CHALLENGE OF PEACE:
> GOD'S PROMISE AND OUR RESPONSE,
> A PASTORAL LETTER ON WAR AND PEACE
> U.S. BISHOPS

Peace in the Modern World: Religious Perspectives and Principles

The threat of nuclear war is a concern of the church, a concern which transcends all national boundaries. The Catholic tradition has offered teaching on the subject of war and peace throughout the centuries and now attempts to articulate a helpful response to an urgent concern. Catholics attempting to discern whether their moral judgments are consistent with the gospel must give serious attention to the moral judgments given in this pastoral letter. (CP 5-7, 10)

Core of Church's Teaching on Peace

At the center of the church's teaching on peace and at the center of Catholic social teaching are the transcendence of God and the dignity of the human person. Catholic teaching on the issue of war and peace is directed toward Catholics, assisting them in the formation of conscience, and the wider civil community, to assist in the public policy debate concerning this important issue.

Theology of Peace

A theology of peace grounds the task of peacemaking in the biblical vision of the kingdom of God and provides a message of hope. The scriptures, written over a long period of time and reflecting many social situations culturally conditioned, offer a variety of perspectives on the meaning of peace. Predominating are an understanding of peace as a right relationship with God and an eschatological sense, the full realization of God's salvation when all creation will be made whole.

"Peace" in Hebrew Scripture

The Hebrew scriptures show violence and war to be a part of the history of the people of God. One image of God that developed was as the One who would protect Israel from their enemies and provide a sense of security. This image was gradually transformed with time, and other activities of God on behalf of Israel showed different perspectives of their God.

Peace is experienced as a gift from God and the fruit of God's saving activity. True peace extends to all of creation and brings harmony and right order. Living in covenantal fidelity to God demanded that Israel put its faith in God alone and look to God for security. Because of Israel's fidelity, God's promise of salvation involving all people and all creation will be fulfilled. (CP 11, 15, 16, 25, 27, 28, 31, 32, 36)

"Peace" in Christian Scripture

In the Christian scriptures, Jesus comes to proclaim the reign of God, calling all to a conversion of heart. In the fullest demonstration of God's reign, Jesus bestows the gift of peace—a peace that the world cannot give. In his first gift to his followers after the resurrection, the risen Lord gives the gift of peace. The disciples recognize their mission to be agents of reconciliation, people who would make the peace which God had established visible through the love and unity of their own communities. (CP 39, 44, 51)

Christians are called to live the tension between the vision of the reign of God and its concrete realization in history. We are a pilgrim people in a world marked by conflict and injustice. Justice is always the foundation of peace. In the "already but not yet" of Christian existence, the members of the church choose different paths to move toward the realization of the kingdom in history. (CP 54, 58-60, 62)

Peace is both a gift of God and a human work, constructed on the basis of core human values: truth, justice, freedom, and love. The church's teaching on war and peace establishes a strong presumption against war, binding on all. But there are circumstances when this presumption may be overridden in the name of preserving peace, which protects human dignity and human rights.

Defense Against Aggression

Christians must defend peace against aggression. The manner in which this defense takes place presents moral options, including service in the armed forces or refusing to bear arms. Catholic teaching sees these two positions as complementary, in that both seek to serve the common good.

Work to develop nonviolent means of fending off aggression and resolving conflict best reflects the call of Jesus to love and to do justice. (CP 73, 74, 78)

Saint Augustine developed what has become known as the "just war" theory. Lethal force can prevent aggression against innocent victims, the need to restrain an enemy who would injure the innocent. But first, every reasonable effort must be made to prevent war.

Catholic teaching has developed a determination as to when war is permissible:

1. *Just cause:* War is permissible only to confront a real and certain danger, i.e., to protect innocent life, to preserve conditions necessary for decent human existence, and to secure basic human rights.

2. *Competent authority:* The decision to use force must be made by a competent authority charged with responsibility for the public good.

3. *Comparative justice:* A decision must be made as to whether the rights and values involved justify the taking of life. Every party to a conflict should acknowledge the limits of its "just cause" and the need to use only limited means in pursuit of its objectives.

4. *Right intention:* A just cause must be the only reason for the war and must continue to be the intention during the course of the war, avoiding unnecessary destructive acts or unreasonable conditions.

5. *Last resort:* All peaceful alternatives must have been exhausted.

6. *Probability of success:* Hopeless resistance should be avoided when the outcome will be clearly disproportionate or futile, with the recognition that at times the defense of key values even against great odds may be a proportionate witness.

7. *Proportionality:* The damage to be inflicted and the costs incurred by war must be proportionate to the good expected by taking up arms. Such consideration is not limited to the material order, but includes the moral and spiritual implications to a society as well. Also to be considered, especially in a nuclear age, is the effect of a possible war on the international community. (CP 81, 84, 86-88, 92, 93, 95, 96, 98, 99)

Proportionality and Discrimination in Targets

The way in which war is *conducted* needs to be continually scrutinized in light of the principles of *proportionality* and *discrimination. Proportionality* demands that when confronting various military options, an analysis be made of the possible harm that might be done and whether a particular military advantage is still justified. The principle of *discrimination* prohibits the directly intended attacks on non-combatants and non-military targets. (CP 105, 107)

Conscientious Objection

Some Christians from the earliest days of the church, moved by the example of Jesus, have committed themselves to a nonviolent lifestyle. The Second Vatican Council in the *Pastoral Constitution on the Church in the Modern World* (79) called upon governments to enact laws to protect the rights of those who adopted the position of conscientious objection to all war. (CP 111, 118)

Nuclear Arms Race

The nuclear arms race highlights two elements: destructive potential of nuclear weapons and the stringent choices posed by the nuclear age for both politics and morals. The danger and destructiveness of nuclear weapons are resisted with greater urgency and intensity. Papal teaching has consistently addressed the folly and danger of the arms race. The possibilities for placing political and moral limits on nuclear war are so minimal that the moral task must be to refuse to legitimate it. The strategy of nuclear deterrence contains serious moral issues, including the economic distortion of priorities for the nation. (CP 126, 131, 134, 136)

For the tradition that acknowledges some legitimate use of force, there are some important elements of contemporary nuclear strategies which move beyond the limits of moral justification:

Counter population warfare: Under no circumstances may nuclear weapons or other instruments of mass slaughter be used for the purpose of destroying population centers or other predominately civilian targets. Retaliatory action (nuclear or conventional) which would indiscriminately take many innocent lives must also be condemned. (CP 147, 148)

Initiation of nuclear war: The situation cannot be perceived in which the deliberate initiation of nuclear warfare, on however restricted a scale, can be morally justified. A serious moral obligation exists to develop non-nuclear defensive strategies as rapidly as possible. (CP 150)

Limited nuclear war: A nuclear response to either conventional or nuclear attack can cause destruction that goes far beyond "legitimate defense." Moral perspective should be sensitive not only to the quantitative dimensions of the issue but to the psychological, human, and religious characteristics as well. The first imperative is to prevent any use of nuclear weapons with the hope that leaders will resist the notion that nuclear conflict can be limited, contained, or won in any traditional sense. (CP 160, 161)

The concept of deterrence, the dissuasion of a potential adversary from initiating an attack or conflict, often by the threat of unacceptable retaliatory damage, has become the centerpiece of the major powers' policy. Two questions need particularly to be addressed:

Targeting doctrine and strategic plans for the use of the deterrent: It is not morally acceptable to intend to kill the innocent as part of a strategy of deterring nuclear war. The principle of *proportionality* would indicate that there are some actions that can be decisively judged to be disproportionate: in a nuclear age, the assertion of an intention not to strike civilians directly, or even the most honest effort to implement that intention, constitutes a policy that is not satisfactory. (CP 163, 177, 178, 181)

Deterrence strategy and nuclear war-fighting capability: Counterforce targeting, while preferable from the perspective of protecting civilians, conveys the notion that nuclear war is subject to precise rational and moral limits, a dubious premise. There is a need to rethink the deterrence policy, to reduce the possibility of nuclear war, and to move toward a more stable system of national and international security. (CP 178, 181, 184, 196)

Specific Steps to Reduce the Danger of War:

1. There is a need for continued work on arms control, reduction, and disarmament.

2. There must be a continued insistence on efforts to minimize the risk of any war.

3. Programs are needed which reduce reliance on nuclear weapons and at the same time work to reduce tensions and the balanced reduction of conventional forces.

4. Attention must be given to existing programs for civil defense against nuclear attack.

5. Efforts must be made continually to develop nonviolent means of conflict resolution.

6. Respect must be given to the role of individual conscience and legislative protection provided for the rights of conscientious objectors. The church does not question the right of the state, in principle, to require military service of its citizens, provided the government shows it necessary. (CP 203, 209, 218, 220, 221, 232, 233)

Working to Shape a Peaceful World

Work must continue toward some properly constructed political authority with the capacity to shape our material interdependence. By a mix of political vision and moral wisdom, states are called to interpret the national interest in light of the larger global interest.

The reality of global interdependence calls us to translate our compassion into policies that will respond to international issues, especially poverty in the world.

There is a moral challenge from our interdependence to shape and develop relationships among the nations that will support our common need for security, welfare, and safety. (CP 241, 243, 263, 273)

The Work of the Church in Promoting Peace in the World

There must be educational programs and the formation of conscience to understand better the issues of war and peace. True peace calls for "reverence for life," a full awareness of the worth and dignity of every human person and the sacredness of all human life. There must be a conversion of heart and mind among all people and a prayerful union with Christ, the Prince of Peace. Conversion should lead us to penance, conforming ourselves more closely to Christ. Each Friday should be a day significantly devoted to prayer, penance, and almsgiving for peace.

Challenges to Peace: Persons and Their Roles Specifically Addressed

To priests, deacons, religious, and pastoral ministers: the cultivation of the gospel vision of peace as a way of life for believers and as a leaven for society.

To educators: to use the framework of the Catholic teaching on war and peace toward the development of a theology of peace.

To parents: to teach their children concerning issues of justice and methods of peaceful conflict resolution.

To youth: to study carefully the teachings of the church and the demands of the gospel about war and peace, and to seek careful guidance in reaching decisions about civic responsibility.

To men and women in military service: to look upon themselves as the custodians of the security and freedom of their fellow citizens, contributing to the maintenance of peace.

To men and women in defense industries: to use the moral principles of this letter to help form their conscience.

To men and women of science: to continue to relate moral wisdom to political reality and to assist the church in this effort.

To men and women of the media: to a certain extent, assist in the interpretation given by the general population in regard to the teachings of this letter.

To public officials: to lead with courage in regard to the issues of war and peace and to listen to the public debate with sensitivity.

To Catholics as citizens: to help within the context of a pluralistic democracy, to call attention to the moral dimensions of public issues. (CP 279, 285, 290, 297, 303, 304, 306, 307, 309, 318, 319, 322, 323)

R E F L E C T I O N   Q U E S T I O N S

1. What do you consider to be the most important rights given to you by virtue of being a human being? Why? What are the most important rights granted to you by the state? Why?

2. How does a society best defend the rights of those who are most vulnerable?

3. Does a country have any responsibility to protect the rights of other countries or cultures?

4. According to Pope John XXIII, there can be "no peace among people unless there is peace in each person." How can Christian communities promote this insight in concrete ways?

5. According to the NCCB's document *The Challenge of Peace,* what is the centerpiece of the Catholic Church's teaching on peace?

6. In what ways did the Hebrew people modify their understanding of God over time in relation to war and violence?

7. The bishops describe peace as a "gift of God and a human work." Explain.

8. Do the norms against nuclear strategies proposed by the bishops still have relevance? Why or why not?

9. How could Catholic citizens, as suggested by the bishops, within the context of a pluralistic democracy, call attention to the moral dimensions of public issues such as nuclear arms?

CHAPTER 7

Care for God's Creation

Humanity is called to a stewardship of all God's creation, that the benefits of the present gifts of creation can be preserved and protected for future generations as well as the present generation. We are called to live in harmony with all God's creatures. The following is a summary of Renewing the Earth: An Invitation to Reflection and Action on the Environment in Light of Catholic Social Teaching, *a statement by the U.S. bishops issued November 14, 1991.*

RENEWING THE EARTH
U.S. BISHOPS

At the core of the environmental crisis is a moral challenge: how we use and share the goods of the earth, what we pass on to future generations, and how we live in harmony with God's creation.

The effects of the crisis surround us: smog in cities, chemicals in our water and on our food, eroded topsoil, loss of valuable wetlands, radioactive and toxic waste lacking adequate disposal sites, and threats to the health of industrial and farm workers. The problems also extend beyond our borders: problems with acid rain, greenhouse gasses, and chlorofluorocarbons.

There are various opinions about the causes of environmental problems. The National Conference of Catholic Bishops adds a distinctive and constructive voice to the ecological dialogue underway, a dialogue which involves a moral and religious crisis. The goals of this statement include:

1. Highlight ethical dimension of environmental crisis.

2. Link questions of ecology and poverty, environment and development.

3. Stand with working men and women, the poor and disadvantaged, whose lives are most often impacted by ecological abuse and tradeoffs between environment and development.

4. Promote a vision of a just and sustainable world community.

5. Invite the Catholic community and all men and women to reflect on the religious dimensions of this topic.

6. Begin a broader conversation on the potential contribution of the church to environmental issues.

Humanity's mistreatment of the natural world diminishes our own dignity and sacredness because we are engaging in actions that contradict what it means to be human.

Effects of Environmental Blight

The whole human race suffers as a result of environmental blight. It is the poor and powerless who most directly bear the burden of current environmental carelessness. Their lands and neighborhoods are more likely to be polluted or to host toxic waste dumps, their water to be undrinkable, and their children to be harmed.

Sustainable economic policies, which reduce current stresses on natural systems and are consistent with sound environmental policy, must be put into effect.

Religious and Ethical Dimensions of the Problem

As a community of faith, we are challenged to understand more clearly the ethical and religious dimensions of the environmental issues. Catholic teaching in this area arises from an understanding of human beings as a part of nature. In elaborating a natural moral law, we look to natural moral processes themselves for norms for human behavior. Nature is not merely a field to exploit at will. We are not gods, but stewards of the earth.

Catholics and all men and women of good will are invited to reflect on the moral issues raised by the environmental crisis.

Christian responsibility for the environment begins with an appreciation of the goodness of God's creation: "God looked at everything he had made, and he found it very good" (Gn 1:31). People share the earth with other creatures. But humans, made in the image and likeness of God, are called in a special way to "cultivate and care for the earth" (Gn 2:15).

To curb the abuse of the land and of fellow humans, ancient Israel set legal protections aimed at restoring the balance between land and people (Lv 25). Every seventh year the land and the people were to rest. It invited the whole community to taste the goodness of God in creation.

Jesus came proclaiming a jubilee in which humanity and all creation was to be liberated (Lk 4:16-22). Jesus is the firstborn of a new creation and gives his Spirit to renew the whole earth (Col 1:18-20; Ps 104:30).

Catholic social teaching provides a developing and distinctive perspective on environmental issues. This teaching tradition upholds a consistent respect for human life that extends to respect for all creation. It encourages a worldview affirming the ethical significance of global interdependence and the common good. It proclaims an option for the poor, giving passion to the quest for an equitable and sustainable world.

The whole world is God's dwelling. Through the created gifts of nature, men and women encounter their creator. Reverence for the creator present and active in nature can serve as the ground for environmental responsibility. Good stewardship implies that we must both care for creation according to standards that are not of our own making and at the same time be resourceful in finding ways to make the earth flourish.

By preserving natural environments, protecting endangered species, laboring to make environments compatible with local ecology, employing appropriate technology, and carefully evaluating technological innovations, we exhibit respect for creation and reverence for the creator.

Only with equitable and sustainable development can poor nations curb continuing environmental degradation and avoid the destructive effects of the kind of overdevelopment which has used natural resources irresponsibly.

In moving toward an environmentally sustainable economy, we are obligated to work for a just economic system that equitably shares the bounty of the earth and of human enterprise with all peoples. Created things belong not just to a few, but rather to the whole human family.

The ecological problem is intimately linked to justice for the poor. The option for the poor makes us aware that it is they who suffer most directly from environmental decline and have the least access to relief from their suffering.

Environmental progress cannot come at the expense of workers and their rights. Where jobs are lost, society must help in the process of economic conversion, so that not only the earth but also workers and their families are protected.

Role of Developed Nations

Regrettably, advantaged groups often seem more intent on curbing Third World births than on restraining the even more voracious consumerism of the developed world.

Consumption in developed nations remains the single greatest source of global environmental destruction. We in the developed world are obligated to address our own wasteful and destructive use of resources.

The key factor in dealing with population problems is sustainable social and economic development. Only when an economy distributes resources so as to allow the poor an equitable stake in society and some hope for the future do couples see responsible parenthood as good for their families. Such development may be the best contribution affluent societies like the United States can make in relieving ecological pressures in the less developed countries. To eliminate hunger from the planet, the world community must reform the institutional and political structures that restrict the access of people to food.

Thus the church addresses population issues within the context of the protection of human life, just development, care for the environment, and respect for the freedom of married couples to decide voluntarily and responsibly on the number and spacing of births.

We must care for all God's creatures, especially the most vulnerable.

Our Catholic faith continues to affirm the goodness of the natural world. A Christian love of the natural world, as St. Francis shows, can restrain grasping and wanton human behavior and help preserve and nurture all that God has made.

Scientific research and technological innovation must accompany religious and moral responses to environmental challenges.

A Christian Response

At the heart of the Christian life lies the love of neighbor. The ecological crisis challenges us to extend our love to future generations and to the flourishing of all earth's creatures. At the same time, our duties to future generations must not diminish our love for the present members of the human family, especially the poor and the disadvantaged.

Christian love forbids us from choosing between people and the planet. It urges us to work for an equitable and sustainable future in which all peoples can share in the bounty of the earth and in which the earth itself is protected from predatory use.

All in the Catholic community are called, along with others of good will, to understand and act on the moral and ethical dimensions of the environmental crisis:

✛ Scientists, environmentalists, and economists are asked to continue to help with the challenges concerning the environmental issues.

✛ Teachers and educators are invited to emphasize in their classrooms and curricula a love for God's creation.

✛ Parents, as the first and principal teachers of their children, must teach them a love of earth and nature, and the care and concern for them at the heart of environmental morality.

+ Theologians, scripture scholars, and ethicists are called on to explore and advance the insights of the Catholic tradition and its relation to environment and other religious perspectives on these matters.

+ Business leaders should make protection of our common environment a central concern in their activities, and collaborate for the common good and the protection of the earth.

+ Members of the church are asked to examine their lifestyles, behaviors, and policies—individually and institutionally—to see how we contribute to the destruction or neglect of the environment and to see how we might assist in its protection and restoration.

+ Environmental advocates are asked to join in building bridges between the quest for justice and the pursuit of peace.

+ Policymakers are asked to focus more directly on the ethical dimensions of environmental policy and on its relation to development, to seek the common good, and to resist short-term pressures in order to meet our long-term responsibility to future generations.

+ Citizens need to participate in this debate over how our nation best protects our ecological heritage, allocates environmental costs, and plans for the future.

The environmental crisis of our day is an exceptional call to conversion and a change of heart to save the planet for our children and generations yet unborn. Only when believers look to the values of the scriptures, honestly admit limitations and failings, and commit to common action on behalf of all the land and the wretched of the earth will we be ready to participate fully in resolving this crisis.

REFLECTION QUESTIONS

1. Comment on the effects of the environmental crisis as seen by the bishops. Are there additional effects that

have developed in the intervening years since the publication of this document that should concern us?

2. What is the "distinctive and constructive voice" that the bishops add to the ecological dialogue? Why is this an important contribution toward some solutions?

3. Who do you believe suffers the most from the burdens imposed by economic and ecological carelessness?

4. What do you believe is the single most important cause of global environmental destruction?

5. The bishops have asked members of the church to examine their lifestyles, behaviors, and policies—individually and institutionally—in regard to ecology and the environment. What might be the results of such a review by a parish or other faith communities?

Appendix

POPE LEO XIII
(1878-1903)

GIOACCHINO PECCI was born in Carpineto (near Rome) in 1810. He came from a family of minor nobility. Prior to his ordination to the priesthood (1837), he studied at Viterbo, the Roman College, and the Academy of Noble Ecclesiastics. He was made an archbishop and sent in 1843 as nuncio to Belgium. In 1846 he was named bishop of Perugia and made a cardinal in 1853.

During the course of his stay in Belgium as papal representative, he traveled to London, Paris, and other industrialized cities and nations, which gave him some insights into the implications of the industrial age. While in Perugia, he attempted to work toward a reconciliation between modern culture and the church, a topic which he addressed in several pastoral letters.

In 1877, Cardinal Pecci was invited to Rome by Pope Pius IX to serve as the *camerlengo,* the chamberlain of the Holy Roman Church, who administers the Holy See when there is a papal vacancy. After the death of Pius IX in 1878, he was elected to the papacy on the third ballot. Although he was sixty-eight years old and of seemingly frail health, he would have an energetic pontificate of twenty-five years. During his time in office, he attempted to address the many social issues that confronted the church, especially in the area of labor and management relations and the defense of the working class. He enunciated a clear policy for workers' rights and trade unions and has been referred to as the "workers' pope." His groundbreaking encyclical was *Rerum Novarum* ("Of New Things") which defended the right to private property and the obligation to pay workers a just wage, as well as the need to honor workers' rights.

POPE PIUS XI
(1922-1939)

AMBROGIO DAMIANO ACHILLE
RATTI, the son of a silk factory
manager, was born in Desio,
near Milan, in 1857. He was
ordained a priest in 1879 and
received three doctorates from
the Gregorian University in
Rome. He taught dogmatic
theology from 1883 to 1888 at
the Milan seminary. From
1888 he worked at the
Ambrosian Library in Milan
until he was appointed in
1911 to the Vatican Library.
He was recognized for his
great language fluency and was
sent by Pope Benedict XV in
1918 as apostolic visitor (eventually nuncio) to Poland.
Because he refused to leave the
country when it was attacked
in 1920 by the Bolsheviks, he
was rewarded by the Polish government with the Order of the White Eagle. In
1921 he was named archbishop of Milan and later that same year was elected
to the papacy following the death of Benedict XV.

Pope Pius XI took as his motto "Christ's peace in Christ's kingdom" and
was a strong advocate for peace against the background of an increasingly dan-
gerous world situation. He favored the active participation of the church in the
life of the world. He also sought to promote peaceful relations between employers and employees, continuing and expanding the social doctrine of Pope Leo
XIII, particularly in his encyclical *Quadragesimo Anno* (1931). Written in the
midst of a worldwide depression, this important social teaching document,
written on the occasion of the fortieth anniversary of *Rerum Novarum,* introduced the important principle of "subsidiarity," where nothing should be done
by a higher agency than can be done better by a lower one.

Pope John XXIII
(1958-1963)

ANGELO GIUSEPPE RONCALLI was born to a family of poor farmers in 1881, the third of thirteen children, in Sotto il Monte, near Bergamo. After studies in the seminaries at Bergamo, he was sent to Rome where he received a doctorate in theology from the S. Apollinare Institute in 1904. He was ordained a priest that same year and was appointed secretary to the bishop of Bergamo, Radini-Tedeschi. Drafted into the First World War, he served first as an orderly and then as a chaplain. After the war, his assignments included being named National Director for the Congregation for the Propagation of the Faith. He also did historical research and writing, including work at the Ambrosian Library, where he met Achille Ratti, the future Pius XI.

Pope Pius XI appointed him to diplomatic service in Bulgaria. Under Pius XII he would serve in France, and in 1952 he was appointed permanent observer for the Holy See at UNESCO. On January 12, 1953, he was named cardinal and on January 15, patriarch of Venice, where he quickly became known for his great pastoral zeal. In October of 1958 he was elected to the papacy. He is particularly remembered for his calling of the Second Vatican Council, which he said was done through the inspiration of the Holy Spirit, for a new and vibrant expression of the faith. His encyclical *Mater et Magistra* ("Mother and Teacher") updated the social teaching of the church as expressed in the encyclicals of Leo XIII and Pius XI, concerning private property, the rights of workers, and the obligations of government. *Pacem in Terris* ("Peace on Earth"), issued in 1963, promoted respect for human rights as a necessary foundation for world peace.

POPE PAUL VI
(1963-1978)

GIOVANNI BATTISTA MONTINI, born September 26, 1897, in Concesio, near Brescia, was the son of a lawyer who was also a political writer. After his seminary courses, taken at home due to his poor health, Montini was ordained a priest in May 1920. He then began graduate studies in Rome. Much of his time over the next several years was spent in the papal secretariat of state, involved in such areas as the Catholic Student Movement. He served briefly as an attaché in the nunciature in Warsaw in 1923. In 1937 he was appointed assistant to Cardinal Eugenio Pacelli, who was then the Secretary of State. When Cardinal Pacelli became Pope Pius XII, Montini worked closely with him.

In 1954 he was appointed archbishop of Milan and spent much of his time attempting to rebuild the area which continued to suffer the devastating effects of World War II. He was especially concerned with the plight of the industrial workers.

After the death of John XXIII, he was elected pope at the papal conclave of 1963, and chose the name "Paul" to indicate his desire to reach out to the whole world as the Apostle Paul had done. He worked to complete the Second Vatican Council, which had begun under his predecessor, and then attempted to steer the reforms introduced by the Council.

Among his efforts at social justice can be included the encyclical *Populorum Progressio* ("On the Progress of Peoples"), which made the case for concerted efforts by the developed nations to assist those countries that were struggling in their efforts toward economic and social development.

POPE JOHN PAUL II
(1978-)

KAROL WOJTYLA was born in Wadowice, Poland, in 1920, the son of a retired army lieutenant and a devoted mother who died when he was very young. As a student in the state high school, he excelled in both academics and sports, as well as having an interest in poetry and acting. After college studies at the Jagiellonian University and work in a limestone quarry and factory during the Nazi occupation of Poland, he began secret studies for the priesthood in 1942. He was sent after his ordination (1946) to Rome for doctoral studies. After completing his degree, he returned to Poland, where he was appointed professor of ethics at Lublin University. In 1958 he was appointed auxiliary bishop of Krakow. On December 30, 1963, he was named archbishop and in 1967 a cardinal.

He attended all four sessions of the Second Vatican Council and was influential in many of the debates, especially on religious freedom.

In October 1978 he was elected pope at the age of fifty-eight. His papacy has been marked by a vigorous defense of the dignity of the human person, a theme often articulated in his encyclicals, including his first, *Redemptor Hominis* ("Redeemer of Man").

In order to contextualize the various papal encyclicals, the following chart illustrates by example some world and domestic historical milestones contemporary with the church documents:

Rerum Novarum May 15, 1891	*Communist Manifesto*, 1841 American Civil War, 1861-65 U.S. Emancipation Proclamation, 1865 *Kulturkampf* in Prussia, 1871 First World War, 1914-18 Russian Revolution, 1917-18
Quadragesimo Anno May 15, 1931	Worldwide financial depression, 1929 Adolf Hitler, German Chancellor, 1933 Second World War, 1939-45 U.N. Charter, 1945
Mater et Magistra May 15, 1961	Cold War, 1945-89
Pacem in Terris April 11, 1963	Second Vatican Council, 1962-65 Cuban missile crisis, 1962 John F. Kennedy assassinated, 1963
Populorum Progressio March 26, 1967	Vietnam War, 1965-73
Laborem Exercens September 14, 1981	Solidarity, labor union founded in Poland, 1980
Sollicitudo Rei Socialis December 30, 1987	Communism collapses, 1989

Centesimus Annus
May 1, 1991

Persian Gulf War, 1991

Evangelium Vitae
March 25, 1995

Apartheid ends in South Africa, 1993
Federal office building bombed,
    Oklahoma, killing 168 people, 1995

The following themes of social justice appear in the readings (**boldfaced**) indicated for a particular Sunday or Feast from the lectionary. The homilist may wish to reference the teaching of the church in the area of social justice in the course of the homily.

Dignity of the Human Person

4th Sunday in Ordinary Time-C	Jer 1:4-5, 17-19 Ps 71:1-2, 3-4, 5-6, 15+17 **1 Cor 12:31–13:13 or 13:4-13** Lk 4:21-30	To love is the Christian lifestyle.
7th Sunday in Ordinary Time-A	Lv 19:1-2, 17-18 **Ps 103:1-2, 3-4, 8+10, 12-13** 1 Cor 3:16-23 Mt 5:38-48	God secures justice and upholds the rights of the oppressed.
8th Sunday in Ordinary Time-A	Is 49:14-15 Ps 62:2-3, 6-7, 8-9 1 Cor 4:1-5 **Mt 6:24-34**	Set your hearts first on the kingdom of God.
8th Sunday in Ordinary Time-B	Hos 2:16b, 17b, 21-22 **Ps 103:1-2, 3-4, 8+10, 12-13** 2 Cor 3:1b-6 Mk 2:18-22	God secures justice and upholds the rights of the oppressed.
The Ascension of the Lord-ABC	**Acts 1:1-11** Ps 47:2-3, 6-7, 8-9 Eph 1:17-23 Mt 28:16-20 (A), Mk 16:15-20 (B), Lk 24:46-53 (C)	The Holy Spirit provides the power needed to do the work of God.
15th Sunday in Ordinary Time-C	Dt 30:10-14 Ps 69:14+17, 30-31, 33-34, 36a+37 or Ps 19:8, 9, 10, Col 1:15-20 11 **Lk 10:25-37**	The Good Samaritan is a model for the Christian lifestyle.

The Community and the Common Good

4th Sunday in Ordinary Time-A	Zep 2:3, 3:12-13 Ps 146:6-7, 8-9a, 9b-10 1 Cor 1:26-31 **Mt 5:1-12a**	*Give your coat to that person who is in need, and be willing to walk the extra mile.*
7th Sunday in Ordinary Time-C	1 Sm 26:2, 7-9, 12-13, 22-23 Ps 103:1-2, 3-4, 8+10, 12-13 1 Cor 15:45-49 **Lk 6:27-38**	*To make peace, use nonviolence and love of enemies.*
Holy Thursday: Evening Mass of the Lord's Supper-ABC	Ex 12:1-8, 11-14 Ps 116:12-13, 15-16, 17-18 1 Cor 11:23-26 **Jn 13:1-15**	*Jesus, the Suffering Servant, washes the feet of the apostles and invites us to be of service to one another.*
2nd Sunday of Easter-B	**Acts 4:32-35** Ps 118:2-4, 13-15, 22-24 1 Jn 5:1-6 Jn 20:19-31	*We are called to live in true Christian community, concerned with others' needs.*
Pentecost Sunday, Vigil Mass-ABC	Gn 11:1-9 or Ex 19:3-8a, 16-20b or **Ez 37:1-14** or Jl 3:1-5 Ps 104:1-2, 24+35, 27-28, 29b-30 Rom 8:22-27 Jn 7:37-39	*The "dry bones" of the church and our own communities can be renewed by the Spirit.*
25th Sunday in Ordinary Time-B	Wis 2:12, 17-20 Ps 54:3-4, 5, 6-8 Jas 3:16–4:3 **Mk 9:30-37**	*To be first before God, it is necessary to be the servant of all.*
29th Sunday in Ordinary Time-B	Is 53:10-11 Ps 33:4-5, 18-19, 20+22 Heb 4:14-16 **Mk 10:35-45 or 10:42-45**	*To be first before God, it is necessary to be the servant of all.*

Rights and Responsibilities

3rd Sunday of Advent-A	Is 35:1-6a, 10 **Ps 146:6-7, 8-9a, 9b-10** Jas 5:7-10 Mt 11:2-11	*The Lord gives justice and liberty and invites us to provide that same justice and liberty to all.*
Sacred Heart-C	**Ez 34:11-16** Ps 23:1-3a, 3b-4, 5, 6 Rom 5:5b-11 Lk 15:3-7	*Leaders have responsibilities to insure that rights are fostered and protected.*
9th Sunday in Ordinary Time-A	Dt 11:18, 26-28, 32 Ps 31:2-3a, 3b-4, 17+25 Rom 3:21-25, 28 **Mt 7:21-27**	*We are called to combine our prayer with action on behalf of others.*
13th Sunday in Ordinary Time-A	2 Kgs 4:8-11, 14-16a Ps 89:2-3, 16-17, 18-19 Rom 6:3-4, 8-11 **Mt 10:37-42**	*Christ invites his followers to take up their cross daily, for it is necessary to lose one's life in order to save it.*
22nd Sunday in Ordinary Time-B	Dt 4:1-2, 6-8 Ps 15:2-3a, 3b-4a, 4b-5 **Jas 1:17-18, 21b-22, 27** Mk 7:1-8, 14-15, 21-23	*Be doers of the word, not only hearers.*
23rd Sunday in Ordinary Time-B	Is 35:4-7a Ps 146:7, 8-9a, 9b-10 **Jas 2:1-5** Mk 7:31-37	*We must always practice what we believe and preach.*

25th Sunday in Ordinary Time-C	**Am 8:4-7** Ps 113:1-2, 4-6, 7-8 1 Tm 2:1-8 Lk 16:1-13 or 16:10-13	*The Lord decries the rich who trample upon the poor and needy.*
26th Sunday in Ordinary Time-C	Am 6:1a, 4-7 **Ps 146:7, 8-9a, 9b-10** 1 Tm 6:11-16 Lk 16:19-31	*The Lord gives justice and liberty and invites us to provide that same justice and liberty to all.*
31st Sunday in Ordinary Time-A	Mal 1:14b–2:2b, 8-10 Ps 131:1, 2, 3 1 Thes 2:7b-9, 13 **Mt 23:1-12**	*We are called to service in the name of Christ.*
31st Sunday in Ordinary Time-C	Wis 11:22–12:2 Ps 145:1-2, 8-9, 10-11, 13b-14 2 Thes 1:11–2:2 **Lk 19:1-10**	*Zacchaeus' story invites us to conversion, repentance, and restitution.*
32nd Sunday in Ordinary Time-B	1 Kgs 17:10-16 **Ps 146:7, 8-9a, 9b-10** Heb 9:24-28 Mk 12:38-44 or 12:41-44	*The Lord gives justice and liberty and invites us to provide that same justice and liberty to all.*

Option for the Poor

2nd Sunday of Advent-A	Is 11:1-10 **Ps 72:1-2, 7-8, 12-13, 17** Rom 15:4-9 Mt 3:1-12	*God liberates and defends the poor and those who are oppressed.*
3rd Sunday of Advent-B	**Is 61:1-2a, 10-11** Lk 1:46-48, 49-50, 53-54 1 Thes 5:16-24 Jn 1:6-8, 19-28	*Christ proclaims good news and liberation to the poor.*
The Epiphany of the Lord-ABC	Is 60:1-6 **Ps 72:1-2, 7-8, 10-11, 12-13** Eph 3:2-3a, 5-6 Mt 2:1-12	*God liberates and defends the poor and those who are oppressed.*
3rd Sunday in Ordinary Time-C	Neh 8:2-4a, 5-6, 8-10 Ps 19:8, 9, 10, 15 1 Cor 12:12-30 or 12:12-14, 27 **Lk 1:1-4; 4:14-21**	*Jesus proclaims a mission to bring liberation.*
7th Sunday in Ordinary Time-B	Is 43:18-19, 21-22, 24b-25 **Ps 41:2-3, 4-5, 13-14** 2 Cor 1:18-22 Mk 2:1-12	*Show regard for the poor and those who are lowly.*
3rd Sunday of Lent-C	**Ex 3:1-8a, 13-15** Ps 103:1-2, 3-4, 6-7, 8+11 1 Cor 10:1-6, 10-12 Lk 13:1-9	*God is liberator and sends Moses to free Israel from oppression.*

4th Sunday of Lent-C	Jos 5:9a, 10-12 **Ps 34:2-3, 4-5, 6-7** 2 Cor 5:17-21 Lk 15:1-3, 11-32	*The Lord hears the cry of the poor.*
Holy Thursday, Chrism Mass-ABC	**Is 61:1-3ab, 6a, 8b-9** Ps 89:21-22, 25, 27 Rv 1:5-8 Lk 4:16-21	*Christ proclaims good news and liberation to the poor.*
Holy Thursday, Chrism Mass-ABC	Is 61:1-3ab, 6a, 8b-9 Ps 89:21-22, 25, 27 Rv 1:5-8 **Lk 4:16-21**	*Jesus proclaims a mission to bring liberation.*
13th Sunday in Ordinary Time-B	Wis 1:13-15, 2:23-24 Ps 30:2+4, 5-6, 11-12a+13b **2 Cor 8:7, 9, 13-15** Mk 5:21-43 or 5:21-24, 35-43	*We are called to share with those who are in need; Christ became poor that he might enrich us.*
19th Sunday in Ordinary Time-B	1 Kgs 19:4-8 **Ps 34:2-3, 4-5, 6-7, 8-9** Eph 4:30–5:2 Jn 6:41-51	*The Lord hears the cry of the poor.*
19th Sunday in Ordinary Time-C	Wis 18:6-9 Ps 33:1+12, 18-19, 20-22 Heb 11:1-2, 8-19 or 11:1-2, 8-12 **Lk 12:32-48 or 12:35-40**	*Jesus calls us to a special concern for the poor.*

20th Sunday in Ordinary Time-B	Prv 9:1-6 **Ps 34:2-3, 4-5, 6-7** Eph 5:15-20 Jn 6:51-58	*The Lord hears the cry of the poor.*
22nd Sunday in Ordinary Time-C	Sir 3:17-18, 20, 28-29 Ps 68:4-5, 6-7, 10-11 Heb 12:18-19, 22-24a **Lk 14:1, 7-14**	*Jesus tells a parable about the need for humility and hospitality.*
26th Sunday in Ordinary Time-C	Am 6:1a, 4-7 Ps 146:7, 8-9a, 9b-10 1 Tm 6:11-16 **Lk 16:19-31**	*The story of Lazarus and the wealthy man shows that we are called to reach out to the poor.*
28th Sunday in Ordinary Time-B	Wis 7:7-11 Ps 90:12-13, 14-15, 16-17 Heb 4:12-13 **Mk 10:17-30 or 10:17-27**	*The wealthy young man refuses Christ's call to voluntary poverty.*
30th Sunday in Ordinary Time-A	**Ex 22:20-26** Ps 18:2-3a, 3b-4, 47+51 1 Thes 1:5c-10 Mt 22:34-40	*We are called to show justice and mercy even to strangers and outsiders.*

Solidarity

3rd Sunday in Ordinary Time-C	Neh 8:2-4a, 5-6, 8-10 Ps 19:8, 9, 10, 15 **1 Cor 12:12-30 or 12:12-14, 27** Lk 1:1-4, 4:14-21	*If one suffers then all suffer.*
5th Sunday in Ordinary Time-A	**Is 58:7-10** Ps 112:4-5, 6-7, 8-9 1 Cor 2:1-5 Mt 5:13-16	*God does not desire empty worship, but a conversion of heart that produces justice, love, and mercy.*
4th Sunday of Lent-C	Jos 5:9a, 10-12 Ps 34:2-3, 4-5, 6-7 2 Cor 5:17-21 **Lk 15:1-3, 11-32**	*Christ associated himself with the outcasts of society.*
18th Sunday in Ordinary Time-C	Eccl 1:2, 2:21-23 Ps 90:3-4, 5-6, 12-14, 17 **Col 3:1-5, 9-11** Lk 12:13-21	*Eliminate all racial discrimination within the community.*
23rd Sunday in Ordinary Time-A	Ez 33:7-9 Ps 95:1-2, 6-7, 8-9 **Rom 13:8-10** Mt 18:15-20	*Our only debt is to have love for one another.*
34th or Last Sunday in Ordinary Time, Christ the King-A	Ez 34:11-12, 15-17 Ps 23:1-3a, 3b-4, 5-6 1 Cor 15:20-26, 28 **Mt 25:31-46**	*Whatever we do to our neighbor who is in need, we do to Christ.*

Reconciliation Service for Justice and Peace

After an appropriate gathering hymn, the celebrant greets the assembly.

Celebrant: May God open our hearts to God's law of love and grant you peace. May God answer our prayers for reconciliation, especially for those times that we have failed to respect the dignity of our brothers and sisters. May God grant you peace and friendship.

Response: **Amen.**

C: My brothers and sisters, God calls us to a true and thorough change of heart. Let us now ask God for the grace of true repentance and a renewed heart. (*Pause for silent prayer.*)

Almighty and merciful God, you have brought us together to bestow your mercy and grace. Open our eyes to see those times that we have failed to acknowledge the dignity and value of each human being and have ignored their needs. Forgive us for the times that we have failed in our duties to love and serve one another. Touch our hearts and return them to you. May your power heal and strengthen us, and may we be recommitted in our baptismal service to be promoters and defenders of your life within each human being. We make our prayer through Christ our Lord.

R: **Amen.**

First Reading

Isaiah 58:1-11

This, rather, is the fasting that I wish: releasing those bound unjustly. . . .

Psalm Response

Psalm 119

Happy are they who follow the law of the Lord!

R: Happy are they who follow the law of the Lord!

Happy are they whose way is blameless,

who walk in the law of the Lord.

R: Happy are they who follow the law of the Lord!

With all my heart, I seek you;

let me not stray from your commands.

Within my heart I treasure your promise,

that I may not sin against you.

R: Happy are they who follow the law of the Lord!

Blessed are you, O Lord;

teach me your statutes.

With my lips I declare

all the ordinances of your mouth.

R: Happy are they who follow the law of the Lord!

I will mediate on your precepts

and consider your ways.

In your statutes I will delight;

I will not forget your words.

R: Happy are they who follow the law of the Lord!

New Testament Reading

James 2:14-26

What use is it if someone says that he believes and does not manifest his works?

Gospel Reading

Matthew 5:1-12

When he saw the crowd, he went up to the hill and taught his disciples.

(A brief homily is given which leads the community to reflect on God's living word and on the responsibilities of living the Christian life.)

Examination of Conscience

1. Have I a genuine love for my neighbor, or do I use them for my own ends?

2. Have I contributed to the well-being of my family by genuine care and concern? Has my example in sensitivity to the needs of others, especially the disadvantaged, been of help to my family in knowing Jesus better?

3. Do I share my possessions with others less fortunate, or do I hoard, accumulating much more than I could ever use?

4. Do I help those who are oppressed by society in any way? The poor? The marginalized? The minority?

5. Does my life reflect the mission I received in confirmation? Do I share in outreach efforts sponsored by my parish, my diocese, and other worthwhile projects and programs?

6. Have I attempted in some way to assist in the church's mission to bring peace and justice to the world?

7. Am I concerned for the good and prosperity of the human community in which I live, or do I spend my life caring only for myself?

8. Have I done violence to another in any way? Have I been respectful of the dignity of other human beings? Do I respect life from the womb to the tomb?

9. Have I gone against my conscience out of fear or hypocrisy?

10. Have I always tried to act out of a spirit of justice and what is morally right?

Celebrant: My brothers and sisters, we all acknowledge that we are sinners and are in need of God's mercy. We are moved to penance and look to live the new life of grace. We admit our guilt and say, "Lord, I acknowledge my sins; my offenses are always before me. Turn away your face, Lord, from my sins, and blot out all my wrongdoing. Give me back the joy of your salvation and give me a new and steadfast spirit."

We are sorry for having offended you, God, especially by our passivity and inactivity when we were called to work on behalf of your gospel but turned aside. Be merciful and restore us to your friendship. Amen.

Now in obedience to Christ himself, let us join in prayer to the Father, asking him to forgive us as we forgive others. Our Father . . . .

> Father, our source of life,
> you know our weakness.
> May we reach out with joy to grasp your hand
> and walk more readily in your ways.
> We ask this through Christ our Lord.

R: **Amen.**

Sacramental confession may be celebrated according to the proper norms.

Celebrant: God and Father of us all, you have forgiven our sins and sent us your peace. Help us to forgive each other and to work together to establish peace in the world. We ask this through Christ our Lord. Amen.

C: May the Lord guide your hearts in the way of his love.

R: **Amen.**

C: May he give you strength to walk in newness of life.

R: **Amen.**

C: May Almighty God bless you, the Father, the Son + and the Holy Spirit.

R: **Amen.**

C: Go in the peace of Christ.

R: **Thanks be to God.**

The following are the sources used for the summaries; some of the translations used did not provide a date when the translation was published.

Papal Encyclicals

John XXIII, *Encyclical Letter Mother and Teacher* (Mater et Magistra), in David O'Brien and Thomas Shannon, eds., *Renewing the Earth: Catholic Documents on Peace, Justice and Liberation,* Garden City, New York: Image Books/Doubleday & Co., 1977.

John XXIII, *Encyclical Letter Peace on Earth* (Pacem in Terris), Boston: Daughters of St. Paul.

John Paul II, *Encyclical Letter On Human Work* (Laborem Exercens), Ottawa: Canadian Conference of Catholic Bishops.

John Paul II, *Encyclical Letter On the Gospel of Life* (Evangelium Vitae), Ottawa: Canadian Conference of Catholic Bishops, 1995.

John Paul II, *Encyclical Letter On the Hundredth Anniversary* (Centesimus Annus), Washington, D.C.: United States Catholic Conference, 1991.

John Paul II, *Encyclical Letter On the Social Concern of the Church* (Sollicitudo Rei Socialis), Vatican City: Libreria Editrice Vaticana, 1987.

Leo XIII, *Encyclical Letter On the Condition of the Working Class* (Rerum Novarum), Boston: Daughters of St. Paul.

Paul VI, *Encyclical Letter On the Development of Peoples* (Populorum Progressio), Boston: Daughters of St. Paul.

Pius XI, *Encyclical Letter On Social Reconstruction* (Quadragesimo Anno), Boston: Daughters of St. Paul.

Pastoral Letters and Statements of the U.S. Bishops

National Conference of Catholic Bishops, *The Challenge of Peace: God's Promise and Our Response*, Washington, D.C.: United States Catholic Conference, 1983.

National Conference of Catholic Bishops, *Economic Justice for All: Pastoral Letter on Catholic Social Teaching and the U.S. Economy*, Washington, D.C.: United States Catholic Conference, 1986.

National Conference of Catholic Bishops-United States Catholic Conference, *Renewing the Earth: An Invitation to Reflection and Action on the Environment in Light of Catholic Social Teaching, Origins* 21 (1991), pp. 425-432.

National Conference of Catholic Bishops-United States Catholic Conference, *Socially Responsible Investment Guidelines, Origins* 21 (1991), pp. 405-408.

National Conference of Catholic Bishops-United States Catholic Conference, *Statement on Capital Punishment, Origins* 10 (1980), pp. 373-377.

U. S. Bishops, *U.S. Bishops' Pastoral Letter on Racism: Brothers and Sisters to Us, Origins* 9 (1979), pp. 381-389.

SUGGESTED READING AND RESOURCES

Campaign for Human Development, *Scripture Guide*. Washington, D.C.: United States Catholic Conference, 1998.

Dorr, Donal, *Option for the Poor: A Hundred Years of Vatican Social Teaching*. Maryknoll, New York: Orbis Books, 1983.

Dwyer, Judith, ed., *The New Dictionary of Catholic Social Thought*. Collegeville, Minnesota: Glazier/Liturgical Press, 1994.

Gremillion, Joseph, *The Gospel of Peace and Justice: Catholic Social Teaching Since Pope John*. Maryknoll, New York: Orbis Books, 1975.

Haughey, John, ed., *The Faith That Does Justice*. New York: Paulist Press, 1977.

Henriot, Peter, Edward Deberri, and Michael Schultheis, *Catholic Social Teaching: Our Best Kept Secret*. Maryknoll, New York: Orbis Books, and Washington, D.C.: The Center of Concern, 1988.

Hollenbach, David, *Claims in Conflict: Retrieving and Renewing the Catholic Human Rights Tradition*. New York: Paulist Press, 1979.

Kammer, Fred, *Doing Faithjustice: An Introduction to Catholic Social Thought*. New York: Paulist Press, 1991.

Kelly, J.N.D., *The Oxford Dictionary of the Popes*. New York: Oxford University Press, 1986.

Machman, Edward, *God, Society and the Human Person*. New York: Alba House, 2000.

Marthaler, Bernard, ed., *Introducing the Catechism of the Catholic Church: Traditional Themes and Contemporary Issues*. New York: Paulist Press, 1994.

Massaro, Thomas, *Living Justice: Catholic Social Teachings in Action*. Franklin, Wisconsin: Sheed and Ward, 2000.

McBrien, Richard, *Lives of the Popes: The Pontiffs From St. Peter to John Paul II*. New York: Harper Collins, 1997.

Mich, Marvin Krier, *Catholic Social Teaching and Movements*. Mystic, Connecticut: Twenty-Third Publications, 1998.

National Conference of Catholic Bishops, *Communities of Salt and Light: Reflections on the Social Mission of the Parish*. Washington, D.C.: United States Catholic Conference, 1994.

O'Brien, David and Thomas Shannon, eds., *Renewing the Earth: Catholic Documents on Peace, Justice and Liberation*. Garden City, New York: Image Books/Doubleday & Company, 1977.

Pennock, Michael, *Catholic Social Teaching: Learning and Living Justice*. Notre Dame, Indiana: Ave Maria Press, 2000.

United States Catholic Conference, Committee on Domestic Policy, International Policy and Education, *Leader's Guide to Sharing Catholic Social Teaching: Challenges and Directions-*

Reflections of the U.S. Catholic Bishops. Washington, D.C.: U.S.C.C., 1999.

United States Catholic Conference, *Sharing Catholic Social Teaching: Challenges and Directions-Reflections of the U.S. Catholic Bishops*. Washington, D.C.: U.S.C.C., 1998.

Weigel, George and Robert Royal, eds., *Building the Free Society: Democracy, Capitalism and Catholic Social Teaching*. Grand Rapids, Michigan: Eerdmans, 1993.

Brothers and Sisters to Us	In November 1979 the U.S. bishops approved and released this pastoral letter on racism which contained many suggestions on how to confront and combat what it called a "radical evil."
capitalism	Economic system that is characterized by the private or corporate ownership of goods with investments that are determined by private decision rather than control by the state. Prices and production are determined primarily by competition in a free market.
Catholic Charities	The largest private charitable organization in the United States, raising millions of dollars to assist in meeting people's basic needs, serving 10,000,000 people annually.
Catholic social teaching	A body of teachings that have been issued by the church, particularly since Pope Leo XIII's encyclical *Rerum Novarum*, which seeks to apply the gospel of Jesus Christ to society's systems and laws so that people's rights are guaranteed.
Centesimus Annus (On the Hundredth Anniversary of *Rerum Novarum*)	An encyclical issued by Pope John Paul II on May 1, 1991, to honor the centenary anniversary of the publication of *Rerum Novarum* by Pope Leo XIII. It includes teachings regarding

	the proper ordering of culture, politics, and economics in society, as well as reflections on then-ature of "person" and "true freedom."
The Challenge of Peace	Issued by the U.S. bishops on May 3, 1983, after extensive consultation, this pastoral letter addresses several issues related to war in a nuclear age. It draws upon a long Catholic tradition regarding violence and war, including the "just war" theory, to help frame a response to the important ethical questions raised in contemporary times about the morality of nuclear war.
chlorofluorocarbons	Any of several gaseous compounds containing chlorine and fluorine used especially in aerosol propellants and refrigerants.
Constitution on the Sacred Liturgy	The first major document of the Second Vatican Council issued December 4, 1963, concerning reform of the Roman Catholic liturgy.
consumerism	A preoccupation toward the buying of consumer goods.
Declaration of Human Rights	Declaration completed by the United Nations Commission on Human Rights in June 1948, containing general definitions of civil and political rights recognized in democratic

constitutions, as well as several economic, social, and cultural rights.

ecology
The science that studies the relationship that exists between organisms and their particular environment.

Economic Justice for All
Written after extensive consultation with many sectors of American life, this pastoral letter issued by the bishops of the U.S. (November 18, 1986) sought to bring the church's social teaching to the area of economics and the concrete realities and problems of the U.S. economy, including employment and poverty issues.

encyclical
A formal pastoral letter by the pope concerning matters of morals, discipline, or doctrine, usually addressed to the universal church.

euthanasia
The practice of killing or permitting the death of a hopelessly sick or injured individual in a relatively painless way.

Evangelium Vitae (The Gospel of Life)
Issued by Pope John Paul II on March 25, 1995, this encyclical offered an extensive teaching on various issues related to life, including abortion, euthanasia, and the "culture of death" present in today's society.

Gaudium et Spes (Pastoral Constitution on the Church in the Modern World)	The last and longest document issued at the Second Vatican Council, reflecting on the nature and mission of the church in contemporary times.
greenhouse effect	The scientific phenomenon in which the earth's atmosphere traps solar energy.
just war theory	A theory developed by the church that attempts to propose when a nation may ethically participate in war. This theory also offers certain limitations on the use of armed forces once a war has begun.
justice, commutative	Fairness in relations between individuals and private groups.
justice, distributive	The fair distribution of creation's goods so that basic needs are met.
Laborem Exercens (On Human Work)	An encyclical of Pope John Paul II issued September 14, 1981, to commemorate the ninetieth anniversary of the publication of *Rerum Novarum*. It provided teachings on labor in its social and spiritual dimensions.
lectionary	The book containing the scriptural readings proclaimed at the Eucharist arranged according to a liturgical calendar.
magisterium	The teaching office and authority of the Roman Catholic Church; also the hierarchy as holding this office.

Mater et Magistra (On Christianity and Social Progress)	An encyclical letter of Pope John XXIII issued May 15, 1961, to celebrate the seventieth anniversary of the publication of *Rerum Novarum*, calling for a greater attention to the implementation of economic undertakings with justice and charity.
NCCB	The National Conference of Catholic Bishops, the organization of the U.S. hierarchy, functioning as the episcopal conference for the United States, empowered to make policy, subject to review by the Holy See.
Pacem in Terris (Peace on Earth)	An encyclical issued by Pope John XXIII on April 11, 1963, within the context of escalating tensions in international relations which had culminated in the Cuban missile crisis. It was addressed to all people of good will and offered the services of the church in helping to relieve cold war tensions with gospel values as a guide to promoting justice and peace.
Populorum Progressio (The Development of Peoples)	Issued March 26, 1967, by Pope Paul VI, this encyclical addressed the disparity in economic development among nations and encouraged the more developed countries of the world to assist those who were in need of greater assistance.

proportionality	The principle that requires that the damage done in a war is commensurate with the good that is expected.
Quadragesimo Anno (On the Fortieth Anniversary of *Rerum Novarum*, On Reconstructing the Social Order)	Issued by Pope Pius XI on May 15, 1931, this encyclical commemorated the fortieth anniversary of *Rerum Novarum* and addressed the mounting economic challenges caused by the Great Depression, as well as the political and philosophical issues raised by the growth of communism and fascism in Western and Central Europe. This encyclical also developed a theory concerning "subsidiarity" (q.v.).
Renewing the Earth	A statement issued by the U.S. bishops in 1991, in which they attempted to present Catholic social teaching in regard to issues concerning the environment.
Rerum Novarum (The Condition of Labor)	The groundbreaking encyclical of Leo XIII, often identified as a landmark and turning point for Catholic social teaching. Issued by Pope Leo XIII on May 15, 1891, it was written to address a myriad of social problems of the age, including questions about labor unions, the dignity of labor, and the need for better working conditions. This encyclical stressed the need for greater collaboration between employer and employee to

A Concise Guide to Catholic Social Teaching

resolve the injustices that were especially experienced by the working class.

Second Vatican Council	The twenty-first general or ecumenical council of the church (October 11, 1962–December 8, 1965) called by Pope John XXIII to promote peace and the unity of humankind.
sensus fidelium ("the sense of the faithful")	The intuitive grasp of the truth of God by the church as a whole, as a consensus.
shareholder	A person who holds or owns a share in property.
socialism	One of a variety of economic theories in which the government has some type of ownership and administration of goods.
Solicitudo Rei Socialis (On Social Concern)	An encyclical issued by Pope John Paul II on December 30, 1987, the twentieth anniversary of Paul VI's *Populorum Progressio*. This document continued the papal teaching on ways to deal with obstacles to development in certain poorer parts of the world that could be assisted by the more economically developed.
Statement of U.S. Bishops on Capital Punishment	Document issued November 1980 in an attempt to show the bishops' belief that in the conditions of contemporary society,

	the legitimate purposes of punishment do not justify the imposition of the death penalty.
subsidiarity	The principle that a higher unit of society should not do what a lower unit of society could do just as well by itself.
totalitarianism	A political theory that the citizen should be subject to the total control of an absolute state authority.
USCC	United States Catholic Conference, the civilly incorporated service agency of the National Conference of Catholic Bishops. It was combined in 2001 with the National Conference of Catholic Bishops to form the United States Conference of Catholic Bishops.

ideology 47, 95
in vitro fertilization 33
Jesus Christ 21, 35, 54, 57, 73, 79, 88
John XXIII 57, 74-75, 101, 115, 127-128
John Paul II 19, 26, 37, 41-43, 57, 68, 77, 84, 89, 98, 129
just war theory 109
justice 13-16, 20, 22-23, 25, 27, 32, 47-49, 52, 54, 58, 60-64, 72-73, 78-79, 81-82,
    87, 92, 97, 102-105, 107, 109, 114, 120, 122
justice,
    commutative 49
    comparative 110
    distributive 49
    social 15-16, 22, 49, 58, 60, 65, 67, 77, 83, 128, 132
labor and the disabled 88
labor unions 87
labor, dignity of 84
Laborem Exercens 77, 84, 130
law,
    economic 58
    moral 35, 58, 119
    natural 35, 102, 104
Leo XIII 13, 41, 57-58, 77, 89-90, 94, 97, 125-127
magisterium 32, 90
management 13, 52, 62, 83, 86, 125
mass media 36, 93
Mater et Magistra 57, 127, 130
materialism 86
minorities, ethnic 105
nuclear arms race 111
nuclear war,
    initiation of 111
    limited 112
Pacem in Terris 101, 127, 130
parish 14-16, 37-38, 54, 75, 97, 123
Pastoral Letter on Economic Justice for All 47, 52
Paul VI 57, 65, 68, 75, 128
Pius XI 41-42, 58, 77, 82, 97, 126-127
Pius XII 59, 127-128
poor, preferential option for
Populorum Progressio 57, 65, 68, 75, 128, 130
poverty 20-21, 27, 48, 50-51, 54, 62, 65, 68-69, 80, 96, 113, 118
private property 58, 61, 66, 74, 82, 90, 95, 102, 125, 127
profit 21, 72, 83, 86, 92
proportionality 110, 112
Quadragesimo Anno 41-42, 58, 77, 82, 126, 130
racism 19-22, 25, 37, 54
redemption, mystery of 96
refugees 70
relativism 29, 35
religious freedom 95, 129